The Melchizedek

King of Salem, Priest of the Most High

The Melchizedek
King of Salem, Priest of the Most High

Vinu V Das

Tabor Press

ISBN 978-1-997541-25-7

Table of Contents

Chapter 1: Who Is Melchizedek?

Few individuals stride across the biblical landscape with so brief a record yet so vast an influence as Melchizedek. Appearing only momentarily in Genesis, invoked poetically in the royal oracle of Psalm 110, and expounded christologically in Hebrews, he stands at the intersection of history, typology, and eschatology. His very obscurity has proven magnetic: a king-priest bearing titles of righteousness and peace; a figure introduced without ancestry or obituary; a stranger who blesses Abram and receives homage from the patriarch of Israel's line. For millennia, interpreters have sensed that behind this terse cameo lies a theological treasure chest—one whose contents illuminate the nature of priesthood, the unity of sacred and civil authority, and the forward-looking heartbeat of the covenant.

Chapter 1 therefore opens the book by probing the identity of this enigmatic monarch. Rather than offering a single, reductive answer, the discussion unfolds the canonical data, historical context, linguistic nuances, and early interpretive streams that converge around him. The goal is two-fold: first, to anchor the reader in what Scripture actually narrates; second, to demonstrate how that slender narrative supports a cathedral of meaning whose spires rise into the New Testament and beyond. By the end of the chapter, Melchizedek's profile will emerge with sharper contours—still mysterious, yet demonstrably coherent within God's redemptive storyline. Such clarity is indispensable before we trace how his priest-king paradigm reverberates through subsequent revelation and Christian praxis.

1.1. Prologue: The Enigma Introduced

1.1.1 Why This Study Matters

The figure of Melchizedek appears briefly yet powerfully within Scripture, inviting readers into a rich tapestry of theological reflection that extends far beyond his few recorded verses. His sudden emergence in Genesis 14 challenges us to consider how God's purposes often unfold through unexpected agents who stand outside familiar genealogies and institutional structures. By engaging this study, readers gain insight into how divine initiative can transcend human categories of lineage and office. Moreover, Melchizedek's dual role as king and priest offers a paradigm for understanding the unity of sacred and secular spheres—a theme that resonates with the Christian calling to live wholesomely before God and society alike. Exploring his mystery also deepens our grasp of Christ's high priesthood, which the author of Hebrews explicitly connects back to Melchizedek's order (Hebrews 5–7). This connection reveals how the New Testament interprets Old Testament types, demonstrating the coherence of God's redemptive storyline across covenants. Engaging Melchizedek therefore equips believers to appreciate the continuity and crescendo of revelation that culminates in Jesus Christ. Finally, this study fosters spiritual imagination, prompting Christians to seek God's unexpected work today in contexts where human systems fall short. Understanding why Melchizedek matters sets the stage for a journey that moves from ancient encounter to contemporary application and invites readers to see God's kingdom breaking into every corner of life.

1.1.2 Scope and Limits of the Chapter

This chapter confines its attention to the biblical testimony and immediate interpretive streams surrounding Melchizedek, deliberately avoiding exhaustive treatment of later mystical or extrabiblical legends. While apocryphal writings and medieval legends have expanded his persona, here we focus on the canonical texts—Genesis 14, Psalm 110, and Hebrews chapters 5 through 7—which form the bedrock for theological reflection (Genesis 14:18–20; Psalm 110:4; Hebrews 7:3). Historical context is sketched only to the extent that it illuminates the original narratives; extensive archaeological debates are reserved for subsequent chapters. Similarly, linguistic analysis will concentrate on key Hebrew terms in Melchizedek's name and titles without diverting into broader Semitic philology. The chapter maintains a Christ-centered hermeneutic, emphasizing typology and fulfillment rather than speculative biography. Although patristic and Second-Temple Jewish readings are introduced here, full exposition is deferred to later sections. This strategic delimitation ensures clarity and coherence, allowing readers to grasp who Melchizedek is within Scripture before exploring the wider interpretive horizons he inspired. By establishing these boundaries, the reader is prepared for deeper study of priesthood, kingship, and eschatological fulfillment in the chapters ahead.

Having established why this study of Melchizedek matters and its defined parameters, we now turn to the canonical portraits that introduce his enigmatic presence on the pages of Scripture.

1.2. Canonical Portraits of Melchizedek

1.2.1 Genesis 14 — The Historical Narrative

In the fourteenth chapter of Genesis, Abram's daring rescue of his nephew Lot sets the stage for an encounter that has intrigued generations: the appearance of Melchizedek, king of Salem and priest of "God Most High." This narrative unfolds against the backdrop of inter-tribal conflict in Canaan, where Abram pursues enemy kings as far as Dan to recover captives and spoils. Emerging at the moment of celebration, Melchizedek brings bread and wine to Abram, a gesture rich in symbolism that echoes ancient Near Eastern hospitality and sacrificial rites. Yet the text elevates it beyond mere welcome; Melchizedek pronounces a blessing over Abram, invoking the name of El Elyon and acknowledging divine victory (Genesis 14:19–20). Abram's generous tithe to Melchizedek—giving him one-tenth of all—further underscores the priestly authority vested in him. The abruptness of his appearance and the absence of genealogical detail heighten the sense that this is no ordinary chieftain but a representative of cosmic authority. Through this brief but poignant scene, the narrative invites reflection on divine blessing, covenantal promise, and the relationship between worship and warfare. The reader is left to ponder how God's priest-king foreshadows an ultimate mediator whose priesthood will transcend tribal lineage. As we move from this foundational episode, the psalmist's prophetic oracle will deepen our understanding of Melchizedek's enduring significance.

1.2.2 Psalm 110 — A Royal-Priestly Oracle

Psalm 110 stands as one of the most influential royal psalms, seamlessly blending kingly authority with priestly function in a single figure whom the psalmist declares "a priest forever after the order of Melchizedek" (Psalm 110:4). Composed in the voice of David, it envisions a messianic king who reigns at God's right hand, shattering opposition and executing judgment among the nations. Yet the psalm surprises the reader by ascribing a priestly role to this king, reversing the typical Israelite model where kings and priests were distinct offices. This fusion reflects an eschatological vision in which perfect righteousness and peace coalesce under one ruler, echoing Melchizedek's combined titles of king of righteousness and king of peace. The psalm's audience would have sensed the radical nature of this dual office, anticipating a future deliverer who would mediate between God and humanity. Jewish tradition often linked this priest-king figure to national restoration and divine presence in the temple. For Christian readers, the psalm becomes a cornerstone for Christology, as the New Testament cites it to demonstrate Jesus's superior priesthood (Hebrews 5:6; Hebrews 7:17). In bridging the Genesis narrative and the Christ event, Psalm 110 amplifies the theological resonance of Melchizedek across redemptive history.

1.2.3 Hebrews 5–7 — Christological Fulfillment

The epistle to the Hebrews devotes extensive theological energy to explaining how Jesus embodies the order of Melchizedek, presenting him as the ultimate high priest whose ministry surpasses that of Aaronic lineage. Beginning in chapter 5, the author underscores that any high priest must be appointed by God and capable of compassion, and then swiftly introduces Jesus as one who learned obedience and was exalted (Hebrews 5:8–9). By chapter 6, Melchizedek is invoked as a guarantee of better hope, anchoring the covenant of promise in an unchanging priesthood (Hebrews 6:20). The climax arrives in chapter 7, where a meticulous argument shows that Melchizedek's lack of recorded ancestry symbolizes an eternal priesthood, contrasted with the temporal descendants of Levi. The author emphasizes that Abram's willingness to tithe to Melchizedek foreshadows the greater honor due to Christ (Hebrews 7:4–10). In tracing the argument, readers gain a panoramic view of how Christ's sacrificial work and intercessory role fulfill the ancient type. Through these chapters, the epistle crafts a seamless theological continuum: from the shadowy figure in Genesis to the definitive revelation in the Son of God. Having surveyed the canonical voices that introduce Melchizedek, the next step is to situate him within his broader ancient Near Eastern milieu.

1.3. Historical & Cultural Context

1.3.1 Priest-Kings in the Ancient Near East

The combined office of king and priest, though rare, finds parallels in various ancient Near Eastern cultures where rulers often assumed religious roles to legitimize their authority. In Mesopotamia, for instance, the Sumerian king-priest function served as both civic governor and chief temple administrator, thereby intertwining political power with cultic oversight. Egyptian pharaohs likewise were regarded as divine intermediaries, performing rituals and claiming descent from gods to maintain cosmic order. Against this backdrop, Melchizedek's dual title resonates with familiar patterns of sacred kingship, yet his narrative retains distinct Israelite monotheistic contours. Unlike polytheistic rulers who mediated on behalf of multiple deities, Melchizedek worships "God Most High," affirming universal sovereignty rather than national pantheons. His brief but potent appearance suggests he serves as a covenantal link between Abram and the one true God, bypassing temple structures yet embodying priestly mediation. Exploring these cross-cultural parallels illuminates why ancient audiences would readily grasp the significance of a king-priest figure. It also challenges modern readers to see biblical theology's unique take on power, worship, and divine representation. With this comparative lens, we can better appreciate both the common tropes and the distinctive features that make Melchizedek's role singular.

1.3.2 Salem and the Early Jerusalem Hypothesis

The title "king of Salem" invites inquiry into Salem's geographic and symbolic identity, with many scholars positing that Salem refers to an early form of Jerusalem. Ancient texts and archaeological strata suggest that prior to David's conquest, the site on which Jerusalem stands was called Salem—a Canaanite city of peace long before Israelite settlement. Excavations on the eastern hill reveal fortifications and domestic structures dating to the Middle Bronze Age, lending credence to the hypothesis that Melchizedek presided over a proto-Jerusalem. The name Salem itself, derived from the root sh-l-m, conveys notions of completeness and wholeness, underscoring the theological theme of peace inherent in Melchizedek's kingship. If Melchizedek ruled this early city, his blessing of Abram gains further poignancy: a foreign patriarch receiving priestly hospitality from the sovereign of a sacred locale. While certainty eludes us— ancient records remain sparse—the convergence of linguistic, textual, and material evidence makes the Jerusalem connection compelling. This convergence invites reflection on divine foreknowledge and the sanctity of places chosen by God. As we move toward a closer look at Melchizedek's names and divine epithets, Salem's legacy as a city of peace will remain a central motif.

1.3.3 Archaeological Hints and Limitations

While archaeology offers tantalizing glimpses into the era of Melchizedek, it also confronts researchers with frustrating gaps. Material culture from the supposed period of Abram— circa early second millennium B.C.—is unevenly preserved around Jerusalem, and excavation permits in the Old City restrict comprehensive exploration of key strata. Pottery typologies and small finds hint at urban occupation during the Middle Bronze Age, but linking these directly to Melchizedek's reign requires cautious inference rather than definitive proof. Epigraphic evidence for a priest-king figure of Salem remains elusive; no contemporary inscription names Melchizedek. This silence in the material record underscores the singular nature of his biblical portrayal: he appears where most other rulers left archived legacies, yet his impact echoes across millennia. Archaeological prudence reminds us to weigh textual and material evidence judiciously, acknowledging both discoveries and silences. These limitations, far from diminishing Melchizedek's significance, push readers back to the biblical text as the primary witness and invite theological reflection on mysteries that transcend historical recovery. With this sobering archaeological context in view, we turn next to unpacking the rich meanings embedded in his names and titles.

1.4. Names, Titles, and Divine Epithets

1.4.1 "Melchi-tsedeq" — King of Righteousness

The Hebrew name "Melchi-tsedeq" combines melek (king) with ṣedeq (righteousness), yielding a title that immediately proclaims divine justice as the foundation of his rule. In the patriarchal context, where tribal chieftains often exercised power through kinship and military strength, Melchizedek's emphasis on righteousness marks a striking theological assertion. Righteousness (ṣedeq) in Genesis is not merely moral virtue but covenantal faithfulness—God's commitment to uphold justice and bless the obedient. By bearing this name, Melchizedek embodies the divine standard to which Abram and his descendants aspire. Ancient Hebrew listeners would have recognized the covenantal overtones, recalling that Abraham himself is commended for righteousness in Genesis 15:6. Thus when Melchizedek blesses Abram, it is the righteousness-king speaking to the faith-champion. Beyond wordplay, the name signals that true kingship aligns with divine justice, foreshadowing prophetic critiques of rulers who abandon covenantal equity (see Isaiah 1:23). This etymological insight prepares us to consider how Melchizedek's other titles complement and expand the portrait of a priest-king serving the Most High.

1.4.2 "King of Salem" — King of Peace

In calling him "king of Salem," the text invokes the root sh-l-m, from which the Hebrew word for peace (shalom) derives, connoting wholeness, welfare, and covenantal well-being. Unlike modern notions of peace as mere absence of conflict, shalom encompasses flourishing relationships between God, humanity, and creation. As ruler of Salem, Melchizedek presides over a community characterized by integrated peace—social cohesion, spiritual harmony, and cosmic order. This dimension of his kingship offers a counterpoint to the martial exploits that dominate Abram's narrative, reminding readers that victory is ultimately measured not only by conquest but by restored relationships. The symbolism deepens when we see Salem as proto-Jerusalem, the future city where God's presence will dwell among his people and where justice and peace kiss (Psalm 85:10). Melchizedek's peaceful reign thus foreshadows the eschatological reality prophesied by Isaiah, where instruments of war become tools of cultivation (Isaiah 2:4). In this light, the title "king of Salem" enriches our understanding of his office: he is not simply a monarch who ensures civic order but a priest-king who mediates divine peace to those who encounter him.

1.4.3 "Priest of El Elyon" — God Most High

The designation "priest of El Elyon" identifies Melchizedek as the cultic mediator for the one whom Abram recognizes as "God Most High." The compound name El Elyon appears infrequently in the Old Testament, but where it does, it emphasizes God's supreme sovereignty above all other deities worshiped in Canaan (Genesis 14:18). As priest, Melchizedek stands at the intersection of divine transcendence and creaturely need, offering bread and wine as tangible signs of God's provision and covenantal blessing. This ritual act signifies that worship belongs not to localized shrines or familial altars alone but to the universal God who reigns over heaven and earth. By honoring Melchizedek's priesthood, Abram tacitly affirms the universality of El Elyon, reinforcing monotheism in a cultural setting rife with local gods. Moreover, the term "priest" here predates the formal Levitical institution by generations, suggesting that true worship of the Most High transcends later sacrificial systems. Recognizing Melchizedek as God's priest invites believers to embrace a form of worship that prioritizes heart allegiance over ritual formalism—a theme that resonates powerfully in the New Testament's portrayal of spiritual worship in the Spirit (John 4:23–24).

1.5. United Offices: Priest-King Paradigm

1.5.1 Rarity of Combined Authority

In the ancient Near East, the fusion of royal and sacerdotal authority was uncommon, yet Melchizedek embodies this rare convergence. Typically, kings exercised political dominion—raising armies, administering justice, and securing borders—while priests oversaw cultic rites, sacrifices, and mediation between deity and community. Melchizedek stands apart by bearing both scepter and censer. His dual office signifies that true leadership integrates governance with worship, reflecting the holistic nature of divine sovereignty. Whenever Scripture later distinguishes sharply between the roles of king and priest—such as in the separate lines of David and Levi—Melchizedek's combined title reminds readers that the ideal ruler is first a worshipper. Ancient audiences encountering this paradigm would have recognized its novelty, elevating Melchizedek beyond mere tribal chieftain. The Bible's decision to preserve only this brief episode underscores its theological weight rather than its political impact. Moreover, the merger of offices prefigures the perfect rule of Christ, who alone fulfills both offices without tension. By honoring Melchizedek, Abram acknowledges that the highest human authority submits to God's ultimate rule. This model invites reflection on modern leadership: whether in church or state, those who wield power should imitate Melchizedek by coupling justice with piety. Understanding this rarity establishes a foundation for exploring how Melchizedek's functions intertwine in practice.

1.5.2 Political & Cultic Functions Intertwined

Melchizedek's activities in Genesis 14 illustrate how governance and worship can coalesce into a unified ministry. After Abram's victory, Melchizedek brings bread and wine—

symbols of sustenance and covenant fellowship—to the returning patriarch. This act is civic in that it honors a guest and commemorates a military success, yet it is cultic in invoking God Most High and pronouncing a blessing. The bread and wine function as sacramental tokens, weaving together communal celebration and divine worship. Politically, Melchizedek reinforces Abram's legitimacy by blessing him in God's name, thereby endorsing his mission. Cultically, he mediates God's favor, showing that every secular triumph depends on sacred sanction. This blending of functions dissolves arbitrary boundaries between public and private piety, teaching that every cultural sphere falls under God's priestly oversight. Throughout the biblical narrative, whenever kings neglect worship or priests ignore justice, prophetic critique ensues. By contrast, Melchizedek's unified ministry becomes a corrective paradigm: rulership sanctifies society only when grounded in devotion, and worship rings hollow without social righteousness. This interplay anticipates the New Testament injunction that believers offer their bodies as "a living sacrifice" and "submit yourselves" to governing authorities, demonstrating the inseparable bond between spiritual and civic obedience (Romans 12:1; 13:1). As we move to consider how these functions foreshadow later covenantal ideals, the seamlessness of Melchizedek's roles challenges us to integrate faith and practice holistically.

1.5.3 Foreshadowing Davidic and Messianic Ideals

By embodying both kingship and priesthood, Melchizedek anticipates the union of Davidic and priestly lines in the ultimate Messiah. The Davidic covenant promises an eternal throne (2 Samuel 7:16), while the Aaronic priesthood mediates forgiveness and atonement (Leviticus 16). Melchizedek's brief reign points beyond itself to a ruler whose authority encompasses both domains without division. In Psalm 110, the psalmist echoes this vision ascribing a priestly office to the Davidic king "after the order of Melchizedek" (Psalm 110:4). Such language signals that the long-awaited deliverer will surpass institutional limitations, possessing a priesthood unbound by genealogy and a kingship marked by perfect righteousness and peace. Early Jewish interpreters saw in Melchizedek a type of the coming age, where priest and king share one visage. Christian theology seizes upon this to affirm Christ's unique office: he reigns on David's throne and intercedes perpetually as priest (Hebrews 7:24–25). Thus, Melchizedek becomes the hinge between Old Testament hopes and New Testament fulfillment. His example encourages the church to expect a Savior who rules with justice and ministers with compassion. As we shift to examine the tangible rituals through which these covenantal promises are enacted, the priest-king paradigm offers a framework for interpreting bread, wine, blessing, and sacrifice.

1.6. Ritual Actions and Covenantal Significance

1.6.1 The Blessing over Abram—Structure and Theological Content

Melchizedek's blessing of Abram unfolds in a compact yet theologically dense formula. He utters two declarations: first, acknowledging Abram's championing of God Most High, and second, invoking divine favor upon Abram himself. This structure mirrors later benedictions where a prophet or priest mediates God's word and blessing to the faithful (Numbers 6:24–26). By addressing Abram as "Blessed be Abram by God Most High," Melchizedek identifies the patriarch's victory as divinely enabled. The subsequent line, "and blessed be God Most High, who has delivered your enemies into your hand," redirects praise to the ultimate source of strength. The interplay of address and doxology emphasizes that human success is inseparable from divine initiative. Theologically, this blessing affirms God's sovereignty over history and confirms Abram's inclusion in God's covenantal plan. It also establishes Melchizedek's own authority to pronounce blessings on behalf of the Most High, foreshadowing the priestly function of representing God to the people. Such a ritual utterance transcends mere well-wishing; it enacts covenantal reality, inaugurating Abram's call to become a blessing to all nations (Genesis 12:3). As we consider how this blessing operates in communal worship, we recognize its enduring significance for liturgy and spiritual formation.

1.6.2 The Blessing over Abram—Transmission of Covenant Promises

Beyond its immediate context, Melchizedek's blessing functions as a conduit for covenant promises that will bear fruit throughout redemptive history. Abram had already received God's initial call and promises at Ur and Haran (§Genesis 12–13§), but in this moment his covenant is ratified through priestly mediation. The act of blessing consecrates Abram for future tasks: possessing the land, multiplying offspring, and becoming a blessing to the nations. In ancient covenant rituals, oaths and blessings sealed agreements between suzerain and vassal; here, Melchizedek acts in God's stead to confirm Abram's covenant status. This transmission underscores the principle that divine promises are advanced through priestly channels—those designated to bridge heaven and earth. The narrative thus models how God's word moves from divine intention into human experience via ordained agents. Recognizing this dynamic invites the church to value responsible stewardship of divine revelation: preaching, teaching, and sacramental acts become vehicles through which God's promises reach and transform lives. As the chapter progresses, we will see how subsequent rituals—bread and wine—continue to embody covenantal presence in ever-widening circles of community.

1.6.3 Bread and Wine as Sacramental Tokens

The presentation of bread and wine by Melchizedek carries layers of meaning that extend far beyond simple hospitality. In the ancient world, sharing a meal often sealed alliances, signified peace treaties, or marked solemn covenants. Melchizedek's choice of these elements situates his blessing within the broader context of covenant meals, where food and drink symbolized mutual commitment between parties. Yet here the elements also point to God's provision and the spiritual sustenance required for covenant fidelity. Bread, the staff of life, signifies God's sustaining grace; wine, the joyous fruit of the vine, symbolizes the abundance of divine blessing. By offering both, Melchizedek communicates that covenant life encompasses both the necessities of survival and the delights of communion with God. These tokens thus become tangible reminders that every step of the faith journey depends on divine generosity. As we transition from this ancient gesture to its later Christian interpretation, the continuity of bread and wine in worship practices will reveal the depth of theological continuity woven through Scripture.

1.6.4 Near-Eastern Hospitality vs. Sacred Offering

To appreciate Melchizedek's gift, we must distinguish ordinary Near-Eastern hospitality from the sacred character assigned by the biblical narrator. Hospitality customs required hosts to provide food and shelter to travelers, often invoking divine protection for guests. Yet Melchizedek's offering transcends mere courtesy: the text highlights his priestly title and the invocation of El Elyon, suggesting that the elements function liturgically rather than domestically (Genesis 14:18). This sacralization recasts hospitality as worship, fusing social custom with divine ritual. The reader is prompted to view hospitality not as peripheral to faith but as an integral act of worship that acknowledges God's lordship over all human relations. In contrast to secular banquets where food and drink serve entertainment or political aims, Melchizedek's banquet elevates the meal into a covenant rite. This reorientation challenges modern readers to see every act of kindness and fellowship as an opportunity for sacred encounter. As we move toward the New Testament's more explicit Eucharistic practices, this early example reminds us that Christian sacraments find their roots in God-ordained gestures of welcome and blessing.

1.6.5 Early Christian Eucharistic Echoes

Although the New Testament does not draw a direct line from Melchizedek's meal to the Last Supper, the echoes are unmistakable. Jesus takes bread and wine, blessing them and declaring them to be his body and blood, thereby inaugurating a new covenant in his sacrificial death (Luke 22:19–20). The structure mirrors Melchizedek's actions: elements of sustenance become symbols of divine covenant. Paul's account in 1 Corinthians underlines the communal dimension of this sacrament, urging believers to discern its body-giving power (1 Corinthians 11:23–26). In Hebrews, the author invokes Melchizedek to demonstrate how Christ's priesthood supersedes the Levitical order, making his once-for-all offering sufficient for salvation (Hebrews 7:27). Through this lens, Melchizedek's bread and wine prefigure the Christian Eucharist not merely as ritual but as participation in the priestly blessing of God Most High. The continuity of ritual tokens across covenants underscores God's unchanging heart to commune with his people through simple yet profound means. As we prepare to reflect on Melchizedek's genealogical silence, these sacramental threads remind us that divine mystery often shimmers through understated gestures rather than grand genealogies.

1.7. Silence of Genealogy: Literary Device & Theology

1.7.1 "Without Father, Mother, or Descent" Explained

The striking description that Melchizedek is "without father, without mother, without genealogy" (Hebrews 7:3) functions as a deliberate literary device rather than a biological assertion. In the patriarchal culture of ancient Israel, identity and legitimacy derived from one's ancestry, recorded meticulously in clan registers and tribal rosters. By omitting any reference to Melchizedek's lineage, the biblical author signals that his priesthood transcends ordinary human succession. This silence invites readers to focus on the timeless qualities of his ministry—uprightness, peace, and divine appointment—rather than on credentials rooted in earthly descent. Moreover, the phrase can imply an endless priestly tenure: if no beginning is recorded, no end need be presumed. Theologically, this proleptic anonymity prefigures the eternal priesthood of Christ, who enters the heavenly sanctuary once and for all (Hebrews 7:23–25). Recognizing this device helps us appreciate that Scripture sometimes withholds data intentionally to highlight deeper truths. In Melchizedek's case, the absence of genealogy becomes a powerful signpost pointing beyond history into the realm of divine, unbroken priesthood.

1.7.2 Timeless Priesthood Motif

The motif of a priesthood unbounded by temporal constraints resonates powerfully in Hebrew thought. While Levitical priests served for life but passed the office to descendants, Melchizedek's ministry stands outside that cycle. The absence of recorded beginning or end creates a literary "eternal present," suggesting that his priestly function is ever-available to intercede on behalf of those who seek God. In Hebrews 7, this motif underscores Christ's superiority: unlike mortal priests who die and are replaced, Jesus lives forever and holds his priesthood permanently. The concept of timeless mediation fulfills the longing expressed in Psalm 110 for a "priest forever" (Psalm 110:4). This eschatological dimension offers believers assurance that there always exists a sin-bearer before God's throne, eliminating doubt about access to divine mercy. The motif also challenges readers to transcend limited understandings of ministry confined to human lifespans. It encourages envisioning a continuity of intercession and presence that stretches from Edenic promise to the consummation of all things. As we contrast this timeless priesthood with the genealogies meticulously kept for Israel's leaders, the theological import of Melchizedek's anonymity becomes ever more vivid.

1.7.3 Contrast with Patriarchal Lineages

In sharp relief to Melchizedek's anonymous pedigree, the patriarchal narratives meticulously trace genealogies from Abraham through Isaac, Jacob, and the twelve tribes (Genesis 25–36). These records establish inheritance rights, tribal

25

identity, and divine promises passed down through specific lines. Such emphasis on descent underscores human participation in God's covenantal work: promises become real in families and generations. Melchizedek's exception to this pattern therefore stands out as a dramatic interruption in the flow of human history. His role does not depend on familial status or tribal belonging but on divine prerogative. This contrast invites reflection on how God often chooses unexpected vessels to advance his purposes, unfettered by human conventions. While Israel's leaders were accountable to ancestral mandates, Melchizedek's authority rests solely on his appointment by "God Most High." The juxtaposition thus teaches that while familial heritage matters for certain covenants, the ultimate priesthood—embodied perfectly in Christ—requires no human pedigree. It is a divine gift administered according to God's will alone. Having examined this contrast, the reader stands ready to appreciate the ways in which Melchizedek's timeless, divinely appointed priesthood shapes the unfolding narrative of redemption explored in the chapters ahead.

1.8. Early Interpretive Trajectories

1.8.1 Qumran's 11QMelchizedek Scroll

The Dead Sea Scroll known as 11QMelchizedek presents Melchizedek as a heavenly deliverer, identifying him with the "Angel of Justice" who enacts God's eschatological judgment. This text envisions Melchizedek emerging in the "year of vengeance" to liberate the righteous and defeat the forces of darkness, a portrayal far more expansive than the Genesis cameo (11Q13 col. 2–3). The scroll's language draws on Isaiah's pronouncements of divine recompense (Isaiah 61:2) and reinterprets Melchizedek as the promised anointed one who inaugurates God's rule in the Last Days. Such expectations reflect a Sectarian community eager for vindication under a priest-king figure who transcends mortal lineage. The pseudepigraphal tradition emphasizes his timeless priesthood, echoing Hebrews' depiction of an eternal mediator (Hebrews 7:3). Yet the scroll also imbues him with cosmic authority, conflating priestly mediation with angelic warfare. This fusion resonates with other Qumran texts that depict heavenly priesthood and angelic hosts serving God's end-time purposes (1 Enoch 90–91). The manuscript thus testifies to a richly developed Jewish imagination that embraced Melchizedek as central to Messianic hopes. By portraying him as both judge and savior, the scroll expands his identity beyond earthly kingship to cosmic sovereignty. Moving from this Jewish apocalyptic vision, early Christians would reinterpret Melchizedek through the lens of Christ's person and work.

1.8.2 Melchizedek as Eschatological Deliverer

In Second-Temple thought, Melchizedek increasingly appears as more than a historical footnote; he becomes an agent of final redemption. Texts like the Damascus Document and the Thanksgiving Hymns allude to a priestly figure who will stand against profane rulers and priesthoods, restoring true worship. This eschatological schema merges with concepts of a "priest of the Most High" who inaugurates God's kingdom on earth. Community expectations centered on a purified temple service, and Melchizedek's eternality suited this role perfectly—he required no earthly genealogy and bore divine authority alone. These Jews believed that, like Melchizedek, the deliverer would annul illegitimate priesthoods and establish rites pleasing to God Most High. The notion of a heavenly priest-king dovetailed with sectarian purity laws, underscoring separation from corrupted Jerusalem worship. Such expectations prepared the soil for Christian claims that Jesus fulfilled and surpassed these hopes. As early Christians encountered these ideas, they recognized in Jesus both the promised deliverer and the superior priest-king "in the order of Melchizedek" (Hebrews 7:17). With these Jewish interpretive streams in view, the Patristic era would further shape Melchizedek's theological significance.

1.8.3 Irenaeus: Pre-Incarnate Christ View

Irenaeus of Lyons, writing against Gnostic distortions, affirmed that Melchizedek prefigured the pre-incarnate Christ, the Logos eternally existing with the Father. He argued that the figure who blessed Abram was none other than the Son, appearing in theophanic form to mediate covenant and covenant-promises (Against Heresies IV.20.3). For Irenaeus, this reading underscored Christ's unbroken priesthood, active even before the incarnation. He connected the typology of bread and wine to Christ's own sacramental gifts in the Eucharist, suggesting that Melchizedek anticipated the new covenant meal (Against Heresies III.18.2). This allegorical interpretation pressed beyond literal genealogy, insisting that the Son's eternal nature matched the anonymous priesthood of Melchizedek. Irenaeus leveraged this view to combat Gnostic claims that Christ's humanity was illusory, demonstrating instead that the Son operated visibly in history to bless and redeem. His exegesis cemented Melchizedek as a Christophany—a pre-incarnate manifestation of the God-Man. This patristic lens deepened the church's confidence in Christ's unbroken mediatorial work across dispensations. As theological reflection matured, other Fathers would both adopt and refine Irenaeus's insights.

1.8.3 Origen: Allegory and Spiritual Priesthood

Origen of Alexandria advanced a multilayered allegorical exegesis of Melchizedek, viewing him as a symbol of the soul's ascent to divine communion. He saw the bread and wine not merely as physical sustenance but as emblematic of the spiritual nourishment Christ provides to the believer's heart (Homilies on Jeremiah 16.4). For Origen, the lack of genealogy signified the soul's birth from above, born of God rather than human lineage. He argued that Melchizedek's priesthood invited Christians to pursue an inner worship that transcended external rites, anticipating John's teaching on worship in "spirit and truth" (John 4:23–24). Origen also identified Melchizedek as a type of the Logos, whose consistent intercession sustains creation. In his speculative cosmology, Melchizedek's timeless figure pointed to the pre-existent Word, through whom all things were made (John 1:3). While some of Origen's allegorical flights stirred later controversy, his treatment of Melchizedek enriched the theological imagination regarding priesthood and Christology. His spiritualized reading paved the way for monastic and mystical traditions that emphasized direct communion with God. As the church moved into the medieval period, these layers of interpretation would inform liturgy, art, and devotional life.

Transitioning from these early interpretive currents, we now turn to competing theories about Melchizedek's identity, balancing historical reconstruction with theological typology.

1.9. Contours of Identity: Historical vs. Typological

1.9.1 Historical Jebusite King Theory

Some scholars propose that Melchizedek was an actual Jebusite monarch reigning over pre-Israelite Salem, grounded in the geopolitical realities of the Middle Bronze Age. They point to archaeological layers at Tell es-Sultan (ancient Jerusalem) indicating urban occupation around 2000 B.C., when Abram's journey is often dated. These historians argue that the absence of genealogical data in Genesis may reflect lost local archives rather than theological intent. They emphasize that Canaanite city-states regularly maintained dynastic records which may simply not have survived. Viewing Melchizedek as a genuine historical figure underscores the narrative's ancient roots, affirming that God engaged with real rulers to advance the covenant. Critics question this theory, noting that Genesis sharply frames his appearance as divinely appointed rather than politically motivated. Nevertheless, the Jebusite hypothesis anchors Melchizedek's ministry in concrete history, reminding readers that theological types often emerge from real events. While this perspective enriches our sense of Scripture's historicity, it coexists with deeper theological readings that transcend mere chronology.

1.9.2 Theophanic/Christophanic Interpretation

Building on Patristic precedents, many theologians maintain that Melchizedek's brief appearance is a theophany or Christophany—a visible manifestation of God or Christ before incarnation. This view highlights his titles and actions as beyond what a human king could naturally perform. The instantaneous conveyance of priestly functions, the absence of ancestral record, and the bestowal of divine blessing all suggest a divine agent rather than a mortal ruler. Proponents cite Exodus 24:9–11, where Moses, Aaron, and elders behold Yahweh yet remain alive, as a parallel for divine appearance in human form. They argue that Genesis 14's narrative is written to reveal God's direct engagement with Abram, foreshadowing the fullness of revelation in Christ. This interpretation prioritizes theological coherence, showing that God consistently interacts with humanity through visible mediators. It also reinforces the unity of Old and New Testament revelation, as Christ's eternal priesthood finds a fitting prototype in Melchizedek. While esoteric to some, the theophanic reading underscores Scripture's conviction that God is neither distant nor silent but actively present in covenant history.

1.9.3 Angelic or Heavenly Mediator Proposal

A third perspective interprets Melchizedek as an angelic or heavenly being sent to minister to Abram on God's behalf. This view appeals to Hebrews 1:14, which describes angels as ministering spirits sent to serve those who will inherit salvation. By extension, Melchizedek's role as both king and priest could align with an exalted angelic office tasked with judicial and sacrificial functions. Supporters point to Daniel's visions, where angelic princes preside over nations (Daniel 10:13), suggesting that celestial beings can embody both political and spiritual authority. The angelic hypothesis accounts for the narrative's supernatural overtones and the absence of human genealogy. It also resonates with Jewish apocalyptic literature that portrays angelic hierarchies governing creation and executing divine decrees. However, critics contend that Genesis labels him explicitly as king and priest, roles traditionally human, and that no angel in Scripture bears such precise civic titles. Nonetheless, the proposal highlights the blurred boundaries between heavenly and earthly realms in biblical cosmology and invites readers to perceive Melchizedek's ministry as part of a broader celestial order.

Having surveyed these competing identity theories, we proceed to synthesize our findings and draw key insights for understanding Melchizedek's role in the grand narrative.

Conclusion

Having surveyed the canonical portraits, cultural backdrop, titular theology, and early exegetical traditions, we may now appreciate why the question "Who is Melchizedek?" resists a tidy biographical answer. Scripture deliberately cloaks him in narrative brevity so that readers will see not merely an ancient ruler of Salem but a living signpost to a greater reality. His righteous reign prefigures a kingdom where justice and shalom kiss; his priestly blessing anticipates a mediator whose ministry is unending; his lack of genealogy serves less to erase his humanity than to spotlight a priesthood unbounded by tribal descent. Whether read historically as a Canaanite monarch, typologically as a foreshadowing of Christ, or eschatologically as a heavenly agent of deliverance, Melchizedek compels us to hold together time, promise, and fulfillment in a single theological vista.

This opening chapter thus furnishes the conceptual scaffolding for the rest of the book. By disentangling fact from speculation and highlighting the multiple dimensions of his identity, we are now positioned to examine how the order of Melchizedek shapes biblical priesthood, informs royal theology, and ultimately culminates in the exalted Son who bears both crown and ephod forever. As we turn to the priesthood in shadow and type, the enigma introduced here will transform into a clarifying lens—revealing how God wove hints of an eternal covenant into the earliest pages of Scripture and how those hints blossom into the full revelation of Jesus Christ, the true King of righteousness and peace.

Chapter 2: Priesthood in Shadow and Type

The journey from Melchizedek's singular encounter with Abram to the formalization of Israel's priesthood reveals a divine curriculum in which shadowed rites anticipate heavenly realities. In the giving of garments and the sprinkling of blood, God instructed a fallen people in the gravity of atonement long before the perfect sacrifice would consummate all shadows (Exodus 28–29; Leviticus 16). These rituals, anchored in a tabernacle structure mirroring a heavenly prototype, functioned as pedagogical tools—teaching faith through symbols, mediating God's presence through fleshly elements, and pointing beyond themselves to the one whose priesthood transcends mortality (Hebrews 8:5; Hebrews 10:1–4). Chapter 2 thus explores how the Aaronic system both upheld divine holiness and exposed its own insufficiency, setting the stage for the superior ministry of the Son "after the order of Melchizedek." By tracing connections between ancient cultic practice, prophetic oracle, and New Testament interpretation, we come to see priesthood not merely as a human office but as a living schema through which God would unveil the fullness of redemption.

2.1.From Enigmatic Priest to Institutional Office

2.1.1 Purpose and Theological Aims

The priesthood represents one of the most profound means by which God reveals both His holiness and His mercy to fallen humanity, and this chapter seeks to demonstrate how the Levitical system originated as a divinely ordained shadow of a greater, eternal priesthood. We aim first to clarify why Israel's ancient rites matter for Christian theology, showing that every garment, sacrifice, and ritual functioned pedagogically to point worshipers forward to Christ's perfect mediation (Hebrews 10:1–4). By examining the purposes behind these ceremonies, readers will grasp how liturgical forms carried covenantal weight, shaping communal identity and individual conscience. We will then articulate theological aims, such as understanding the continuity between Old and New Covenants and appreciating the depth of Christ's fulfillment of the typological structures. A major goal is to equip the church today to value historic liturgies not as ends in themselves but as trustworthy signposts directing faith toward God's ultimate self-revelation in the Son. Along the way, we address potential misunderstandings—whether seeing the Law as obsolete or trivializing its moral demands—by situating Israel's priesthood within redemptive history. Through this theological lens, readers will discover that the Levitical system, while temporary, bore enduring significance for understanding God's character, human sinfulness, and the cost of redemption. The chapter also establishes criteria for evaluating contemporary worship practices, encouraging discernment between timeless principles and cultural expressions. Ultimately, clarifying these purposes prepares us to trace how the order of Melchizedek undergirds and transcends Israel's shadow priesthood, revealing the unchanging heart of God across covenants.

2.1.2 Methodological Approach: Typology, History, and Canon

To navigate the complexity of ancient priesthood, we adopt a threefold methodology that honors both historical context and theological coherence. First, typology allows us to read Israel's rituals as foreshadows ("types") of Christ's once-for-all sacrifice and eternal priesthood (Colossians 2:17). We pay careful attention to how New Testament writers quote and reinterpret Old Testament ceremonies, ensuring that our typological readings align with the canonical use of these texts. Second, historical analysis grounds our study in the ancient Near Eastern milieu, comparing Israel's cultic arrangements with those of neighboring cultures to highlight distinctive features (see Exodus 28 for priestly garments in context). By reconstructing the social and religious settings of Egypt, Mesopotamia, and Canaan, we avoid ahistorical generalizations and appreciate the specificity of God's self-disclosure. Third, canonical theology integrates these findings within the broader sweep of Scripture, tracing the progression from Genesis through Revelation to assess how priestly themes evolve and converge in Christ. We resist reading Leviticus in isolation, instead situating its prescriptions alongside prophetic critiques and wisdom reflections to capture their intended function within Israel's worship life. Throughout, careful exegesis ensures fidelity to the original Hebrew and Greek terms, and cross-referencing the Pentateuchal instructions with New Testament commentary safeguards against eisegesis. This balanced approach enables us to honor both the ancient Israelite context and the church's confession that the Law's shadows point inevitably to Christ's substance (Hebrews 10:1). Having set this methodological foundation, we now turn to explore the broader concept of priesthood in the ancient Near East.

2.2. The Concept of Priesthood in the Ancient Near East

2.2.1 Comparative Cultic Roles among Egypt, Mesopotamia, and Canaan

In the ancient Near East, priesthood often served as an extension of royal power, yet its expression varied significantly across Egypt, Mesopotamia, and Canaan. Egyptian priests functioned as custodians of temple wealth and ritual specialists ensuring ma'at—cosmic order—through daily offerings and elaborate liturgies dedicated to deities such as Amun-Ra and Isis. Their elaborate garments, temple architecture, and strict purity codes signaled both access to and distance from the divine presence. In Mesopotamia, the Sumerian and Babylonian priesthoods managed sacred precincts where gods like Enlil and Marduk received sacrifices to secure agricultural fertility and political stability. These priests performed incantations and divination rituals, interpreting omens to guide city-state policies. Canaanite priests, by contrast, served a pantheon of tribal deities, with local high places and altars catering to Baal, El, and Asherah. These cults often involved sacrificial feasts and fertility rituals—practices explicitly forbidden in Israel (Deuteronomy 12:2–4). By comparing these systems, we see that priestly offices routinely combined civic and sacred functions, but in polytheistic settings these functions reinforced local power and social cohesion rather than pointing to universal redemption. Israel's priesthood, as we will see, retains structural similarities—altar, sacrifice, temple service—yet diverges fundamentally in its exclusive devotion to Yahweh and its covenantal framework. This comparative lens illuminates how God reshaped common cultic forms to serve His unique purposes, setting the stage for Israel's monotheistic re-orientation of priesthood.

2.2.2 Israel's Distinctive Monotheistic Re-orientation

Israel's priesthood emerges not as a mere imitation of Canaanite or Egyptian models but as a radical re-interpretation in light of Yahweh's self-revelation at Sinai. When Moses ascends Mount Sinai, God proclaims, "I am the Lord your God, who brought you out of Egypt" (Exodus 20:2), establishing a covenant that transforms former slaves into a priestly kingdom and holy nation (Exodus 19:6). Unlike regional cults serving multiple deities for communal prosperity, Israel's priests mediated between a singular, transcendent God and His people, calling them to ethical and ritual holiness. This monotheistic shift infused every ritual with moral import: atonement required blood, not for appeasing capricious gods, but for satisfying divine justice and maintaining covenant fellowship (Leviticus 17:11). Tabernacle regulations—such as the separation of holy from common, clean from unclean—embodied God's transcendence and demanded community sanctification. The explicit prohibition of images (Exodus 20:4–5) further distinguished Israel's worship, privileging word over icon. In consecrating Aaron and his sons, God established a hereditary priesthood bound to a covenant stipulating both privilege and accountability (Numbers 3:10). This monotheistic re-orientation thus recast familiar cultic structures into conduits of gospel truth, foreshadowing the singular mediation of Christ. As the nation matured, prophetic voices would challenge deviations from this ideal, reaffirming the exclusive claims of Yahweh and His appointed priests. Transitioning from Israel's distinct framework, we now turn to the concrete institution of the Aaronic priesthood itself.

2.3. The Aaronic Priesthood Instituted

2.3.1 Genealogical Foundations: Levi to Aaron (Exodus 28–29)

The establishment of the Aaronic line as God's designated priesthood roots itself in tribal ancestry, tracing through Levi to Aaron and his sons as prescribed in Exodus 28–29. This genealogy functions as more than a biological record; it symbolizes divine choice, illustrating how God selects individuals and families to serve His redemptive purposes. The Levites, set apart for temple service due to their loyalty during the golden calf incident (Exodus 32:26–29), receive a "vocation by proxy"—their descendants inherit both privilege and obligation. Aaron's consecration involves ritual washing, clothing with sacred garments, anointing with oil, and sacrificial offerings, all signifying his sanctification for holy service (Exodus 29:4–9). These rites underscore that priestly authority depends on divine commissioning rather than personal merit. Moreover, the genealogical emphasis conveys stability and continuity: successive generations maintain the worship patterns foundational to Israel's identity. Yet this inheritance also carries weighty responsibility, as priests are held to higher moral standards and liable for communal atonement (Leviticus 10:1–3). While genealogies in Scripture sometimes legitimize political claims, here they validate spiritual offices, grounding the tabernacle's rituals in God's redemptive covenant. As we examine the consecration rituals and garments in the next section, the significance of Aaron's lineage will deepen our appreciation of the interplay between human heritage and divine calling.

2.3.2 Consecration Rituals and Priestly Garments

The consecration of Aaron and his sons unfolds as a multi-stage ceremony designed to set them apart for "holy to the Lord" service (Exodus 28:41). First, they undergo ceremonial washing, symbolizing purification from ordinary status. Next, Aaron dons the linen tunic, sash, robe of the ephod, breastpiece, and turban—each garment embroidered with gold, blue, purple, and scarlet threads. The breastpiece, containing twelve precious stones, represents the twelve tribes, indicating that the priest bears Israel's identity before God (Exodus 28:15–21). The elaborate headdress and gold plate inscribed "Holy to the Lord" atop the turban proclaim divine ownership. Anointing oil poured over Aaron's head sanctifies him, marking him as chosen by God and sealed by the Spirit (Exodus 29:7). The ritual then advances to sacrificial offerings: bull and ram sacrifices accompany the vesting rites,

38

with blood applied to garments and altar to signify life given for atonement (Leviticus 8:23–24). These multi-sensory elements—visual splendor, aromatic incense, tactile oil—imbue the worship experience with profound gravity. Consecration not only transforms men into priests but also educates the community about God's holiness, the cost of mediation, and the sacredness of covenant fellowship. Recognizing these intricate prescriptions foreshadows the perfect, once-for-all consecration of Christ, whose priesthood requires no successive investiture. As we move to daily temple service, the ritual garments remain in view as emblematic of perpetual sanctity.

2.3.3 Daily Temple Service and Sacrificial Taxonomy

Once consecrated, Aaron and his descendants embark on rigorous temple duties, offering morning and evening sacrifices without fail (Exodus 29:38–42). These continual offerings include the burnt offering (olah), grain offering (minchah), sin offering (chatat), guilt offering (asham), and peace offering (shelamim), each serving distinct purposes within the covenant community. The burnt offering symbolizes total consecration, ascending to God in fragrant smoke; the grain offering acknowledges His provision; the sin and guilt offerings address unintentional transgressions restoring fellowship; the peace offering fosters communal communion in meal-sharing contexts. Priests carefully follow detailed instructions regarding animal selection, oil and frankincense use, and the disposition of blood and fat (Leviticus 1–7). Their service anchors the rhythm of Israelite worship, reminding the people daily of dependence on divine mercy and holiness. This sacrificial taxonomy trains worshipers in the seriousness of sin, the necessity of atonement, and the joy of restored relationship. The regularity of these rites contrasts with the singular encounter of Melchizedek, highlighting the provisional nature of the Aaronic ministry. As we examine the climactic Day of Atonement next, the daily service sets the background for Israel's deepest crisis of sin and need for reconciliation.

2.3.4 High-Priestly Duties: Day of Atonement (Leviticus 16)

The Day of Atonement (Yom Kippur) stands as the pinnacle of Israel's sacrificial calendar, when the high priest alone enters the Most Holy Place to make atonement for himself, his household, and the entire nation (Leviticus 16:2–3). This solemn ritual begins with elaborate preparations: the high priest bathes, dons specialized linen garments, and offers a bull as a sin offering for his own iniquities (Leviticus 16:4–6). He then casts lots over two goats, presenting one to the Lord as a sin offering and sending the other—the scapegoat—into the wilderness bearing Israel's confessed sins (Leviticus 16:7–10). The blood of the sacrificial goat is carried behind the curtain and sprinkled on and before the mercy seat, symbolizing the cleansing of the sanctuary itself (Leviticus 16:14–15). The ritual culminates in the removal of sin from the camp by releasing the scapegoat, which illustrates the communal dimension of atonement. Only after these rites does the high priest resume his garments of glory to offer burnt offerings, marking a restored relationship between God and His people. Yom Kippur's unparalleled access to the divine presence underscores both the severity of sin and the lengths to which God goes to maintain covenant fellowship. Theologically, this foreshadows Christ's one-time entry into the heavenly sanctuary with His own blood to secure eternal redemption (Hebrews 9:11–12). As we reflect on mortality and moral failure next, the Day of Atonement provides a vivid backdrop for understanding the inadequacy of repeated sacrifices.

2.3.5 Limitations of Mortality and Moral Failure

Despite the careful design of genealogies, consecrations, and daily offerings, Israel's priesthood repeatedly demonstrated its limitations through human mortality and moral failure. Priests who succumbed to greed, sexual immorality, or idolatry brought scandal rather than sanctification, violating the holiness they were meant to uphold (1 Samuel 2:12–17). Nadab and Abihu's unauthorized fire resulted in instant death, testifying to the peril of approaching God outside prescribed boundaries (Leviticus 10:1–2). Even at the Day of Atonement, the repetition of sacrifices year after year highlighted the inability of animal blood to remove sin permanently (Hebrews 10:3). The mortality of priests meant that each generation risked losing faithful mediators, creating vulnerability in Israel's worship life. Prophets like Malachi chastised the priests for offering blemished sacrifices and perverting justice (Malachi 1:6–14; 2:1–9), revealing a systemic breakdown in covenant fidelity. These failures underscore the sobering truth that human institutions cannot bear the full weight of divine holiness. Yet they also sharpen the longing for a priest-king whose life is indestructible and whose sacrifice requires no repetition. Recognizing these limitations naturally leads us to revisit Melchizedek's precursory role as a non-Levitical, timeless priest-king—our next focal point.

2.4. Pre-Mosaic Priesthood: Melchizedek's Precedence

2.4.1 Family Altars versus Universal Priest-King

In the pre-Mosaic era, patriarchs like Noah, Abraham, and Isaac built altars at critical junctures of covenant encounter, yet these were family-based and localized acts of worship rather than institutional offices (Genesis 12:7; 13:18). Such altars symbolized individual fellowship with God but lacked the continuity and public authority of a centralized priesthood. By contrast, Melchizedek emerges as a universal priest-king serving "God Most High," transcending tribal boundaries and prefiguring a priesthood that embraces all peoples (Genesis 14:18). His abrupt appearance without prior lineage disrupts the paradigm of familial worship, introducing a covenantal mediator who stands independent of tribal structures. This shift from private altars to a public office signals God's intention to expand worship beyond the confines of family and clan. While later Israel centralized worship at the tabernacle and temple, Melchizedek's ministry points to a priesthood rooted in divine appointment rather than human institution. His universal role invites reflection on the church's mission to bear blessing to the nations, echoing Abram's call to be a "blessing to all families of the earth" (Genesis 12:3). As we move to examine non-Levitical paradigms, Melchizedek's example challenges any narrow vision of worship confined to ethnic or geographical boundaries.

2.4.2 Blessing without Genealogy: A Non-Levitical Paradigm

Melchizedek's blessing of Abram and Abram's tithe to him establish a prototype of priestly authority rooted solely in divine commissioning, devoid of familial credentials (Genesis 14:20). This non-Levitical paradigm contrasts sharply with the later requirement that only descendants of Aaron serve in the tabernacle (Numbers 18:1–7). The absence of recorded ancestry in Melchizedek's case underscores his role as a theologically driven figure rather than a historically grounded one, inviting readers to focus on his functions more than his pedigree. His independence from the Levitical line anticipates the superior priesthood of Christ, which requires no human ancestry but originates in divine initiative (Hebrews 7:23–28). This paradigm also foreshadows the inclusion of Gentiles into the people of God, as the priesthood extends beyond Israel's tribal boundaries to embrace all nations reconciled through Him. By examining this anomaly, we appreciate how God reserves the right to institute new forms of ministry when existing systems prove insufficient. Melchizedek's non-genealogical priesthood thus becomes a paradigm for understanding how God can transcend institutional norms to fulfill His redemptive purposes, a theme developed fully in the New Testament's presentation of Christ.

2.4.3 Implications for Covenant Universality

The existence of a priest-king who operates outside Israel's tribal confines carries profound implications for the universality of God's covenant promises. Melchizedek's ministry to Abram—a foreigner in Canaan—anticipates the gospel's expansion to Gentile peoples, signaling that salvation and blessing are not limited to ethnic Israel (Genesis 14:19). This universality contrasts with the earlier promise to Abraham's descendants but aligns with the later fulfillment in Christ, who breaks down dividing walls and creates one new humanity (Ephesians 2:14–16). By honoring Melchizedek, Abram foreshadows the inclusion of non-Israelites into worship at the Father's table, paving the way for the multiethnic church. Furthermore, covenant universality underlies the church's understanding of the priesthood of all believers (1 Peter 2:9), where every recipient of grace participates in mediating God's truth to the world. Recognizing these implications deepens our grasp of the gospel's expansive reach and challenges any parochial understanding of God's people. As we conclude this chapter, we see that Melchizedek's model beckons us beyond shadow ceremonies toward a faith that embraces all nations in the unending priesthood of Christ.

2.5. Priesthood in Shadow: Typological Structures within Torah

2.5.1 Tabernacle Architecture as Earthly Copy of the Heavenly Pattern

The design of the Tabernacle, as revealed to Moses on Mount Sinai, served as a tangible blueprint of a heavenly sanctuary that dwells eternally before God's throne (Exodus 25:9; Hebrews 8:5). Its outer courtyard, holy place, and Most Holy Place correspond to realms of approach to the divine, teaching worshipers about increasing degrees of holiness and the necessity of mediation. The bronze altar and laver in the courtyard symbolize purification and the costliness of atonement, reminding Israel that access to God requires both cleansing and sacrifice. Within the holy place, the table of showbread, lampstand, and altar of incense communicate ongoing fellowship, illumination by the Spirit, and the value of prayer ascending like perfumed smoke. The veil separating the holy place from the Most Holy Place foreshadows the ultimate tearing of Christ's flesh to grant human access to God (Matthew 27:51). The ark of the covenant, hidden behind the veil, contained the tablets of the Law, Aaron's rod, and manna—signifying the convergence of God's word, priestly authority, and providential care. Every measurement, material, and color choice in the Tabernacle paralleled descriptions in prophetic visions of God's throne room (Ezekiel 1; Revelation 4). Priests who entered its chambers did so on God's terms, learning through ritual geometry and symbolic elements that their ministry pointed beyond ritual to reality. The Tabernacle thus functioned as a pedagogical model: a corporeal sermon about God's presence and the means to approach Him. By understanding this earthly copy, we prepare to appreciate the perfect, non-made-with-hands sanctuary where Christ ministers eternally (Hebrews 9:11–12).

2.5.2 Garments of "Glory and Beauty" as Mediatorial Signs

The priestly vestments prescribed in Exodus 28–29 carried profound semiotic weight, each article conveying aspects of mediation between a holy God and His covenant people. The breastpiece, adorned with twelve precious stones, signified that the high priest bore Israel's twelve tribes before the Lord, intertwining communal identity with sacerdotal responsibility. The ephod's intricate embroidery and gold settings spoke of the wealth of God's provision and the gravity of representing His people. The robe of the ephod, with its hem of golden bells and pomegranates, announced the priest's arrival before God in audible terms, underscoring that his service was both visible and proclaimed. The sash and tunic of fine linen mirrored purity and righteousness, reminding the priest—and by extension the worshipers—that access to God demands moral and ceremonial holiness (Leviticus 16:4). The turban's golden plate inscribed "Holy to the Lord" functioned as a perpetual proclamation of divine ownership over the mediator. These garments were more than mere robes; they enacted the theological truth that God's representative must be adorned in attributes reflecting divine character. As the chapter moves forward, we'll see how these symbols find deeper fulfillment in Christ, who alone perfectly embodies the glory and beauty required to reconcile humanity to God.

2.5.3 Sacrificial Blood and the Logic of Substitution

Israel's sacrificial system revolved around the motif of substitution, where the life of an unblemished animal was offered in place of the worshiper's own life, symbolizing the transfer of guilt and the satisfying of divine justice (Leviticus 17:11). The shedding of blood on the altar signified that life, the bearer of the soul, belonged to God and must be reckoned with in covenant fellowship. Different offerings addressed distinct categories of human condition: sin offerings covered unintentional transgressions, guilt offerings made restitution for specific wrongs, and burnt offerings expressed total surrender. The meticulous priests' handling of blood—sprinkling it on the horns of the altar and, on the Day of Atonement, within the holy of holies—emphasized that divine hubris must be met with death to restore relational equilibrium (Leviticus 4; 16). This logic of substitution, while powerful, also highlighted the temporary efficacy of each sacrifice, as ongoing transgressions necessitated repeated rites. The ritual underscored that the holiness gap between God and His people could not be bridged by human effort alone but required a vicarious exchange. As we proceed to explore the scapegoat motif, we will see how the sacrificial system both revealed God's justice and magnified the need for a once-for-all substitutional priesthood fulfilled in Christ (Hebrews 10:10).

2.5.4 Scapegoat and Sin Removal Motifs

The Day of Atonement introduced the powerful image of the scapegoat, upon which the community's confessed sins were symbolically placed before the animal was sent into the wilderness (Leviticus 16:21–22). This act dramatized the removal of sin from the camp, illustrating that forgiveness not only satisfies divine justice but also restores relational and communal purity. The dichotomy of two goats—one sacrificed and one released—emphasized both propitiation and expiation: God's wrath is turned away in the slain offering, and the stain of sin is carried far from the people by the living goat. Priests performing these rites communicated that ultimate cleansing involves both blood and banishment, reflecting a multidimensional atonement. The wilderness sending evokes themes from Deuteronomy's sin offerings, where removing defilement involved carrying guilt beyond the camp (Numbers 19). Ritual texts and prophetic literature later repurposed this motif to anticipate a cleansing eradication of iniquity in the eschaton (Isaiah 53:6; Ezekiel 36:33–34). As we transition to how priestly patterns converge in prophetic oracle, the scapegoat's drama prepares us to recognize the fuller, permanent removal of sin through Christ's sacrificial work, who both bears our transgressions and washes us thoroughly.

2.6. King-Priest Convergence in Old-Testament Prophecy

2.6.1 Psalm 110: Royal-Priestly Oracle and Oath

Psalm 110, attributed to David, stands as a singular mingling of kingship and priesthood, declaring, "You are a priest forever after the order of Melchizedek" (Psalm 110:4). The psalm's opening address, "Sit at my right hand," affirms the king's divine appointment and authority to rule over enemies and nations (Psalm 110:1–2). Yet the sudden shift to a priestly vocation subverts Israel's customary separation of royal Davidic line and Levitical priesthood, heralding an eschatological figure who unites both functions. The imagery of a purified people offered like a freewill offering at the break of dawn (Psalm 110:3) suggests that worship and governance operate in tandem, testifying to God's reign through both justice and ritual holiness. The citation of this oracle in Hebrews frames Christ as the fulfillment of this dual office (Hebrews 5:6; 7:17), anchoring the narrative that his intercession stems from legitimate priesthood and supreme kingship. Early Jewish interpreters connected the psalm to national restoration; Christian exegesis transcends that to view the Messiah's cosmic reign and mediatorial work. Recognizing Psalm 110's oracle prepares us to see how later prophets carry forward the hope for a unified king-priest who embodies covenant faithfulness and sacrificial love.

2.6.2 Zechariah 6:12–13—The Crowning of Joshua the High Priest

In Zechariah 6, the prophet receives a vision of four chariots and golden crowns, culminating in an oracle: "Behold the man whose name is the Branch... he shall branch out from his place and build the temple of the Lord... and he shall bear royal honor" (Zechariah 6:12–13). This passage depicts Joshua the high priest receiving a crown, intertwining priestly duties with royal imagery. The "Branch" title evokes messianic expectations tied to Davidic and priestly lines, suggesting a future figure who merges both roles. Unlike the purely royal connotations in other texts, Zechariah's crowning of a priest foreshadows a hybrid office, intimating that spiritual and political leadership converge in God's restored community. The vision's emphasis on building the temple also links the priest-king to sanctuary renewal, pointing to eschatological worship under messianic governance. While Joshua himself did not fulfill these lofty prophetic promises, the pattern sets a typological stage for seeing Jesus as the true Branch who renovates the cosmic temple. Transitioning from this prophetic symbol, we will explore Ezekiel's visions next, where the ideal prince and the sanctuary converge in vivid detail.

2.6.3 Ezekiel's Eschatological Prince and Sanctuary Renewal

Ezekiel's prophecies envision a restored land governed by an "anointed prince" who rules with justice and whose presence sanctifies the renewed temple (Ezekiel 45:22; 46:2). This eschatological prince combines kingly authority with liturgical oversight, overseeing offerings, teaching justice, and welcoming the people's worship. Ezekiel 43 describes the return of divine glory to the temple, indicating that this figure operates under a theocratic paradigm where priestly and royal functions emanate from God's enthroned presence. The prince's role in apportioning land, regulating sabbaths, and establishing purifying rites further underscores the inseparability of governance and worship in the new covenant community (Ezekiel 46:18–24). While distinct from Levitical priests, he oversees their service, pointing to a superior mediator whose authority surpasses formal priesthood. By situating the prince within the renewed sanctuary, Ezekiel prefigures the comprehensive reign of the Messiah, who embodies both offices and inaugurates the ultimate temple—God dwelling with humanity (Revelation 21:3). As we shift to intertestamental literature, these prophetic blueprints will inform how Jewish hopes coalesced around a priest-king figure.

2.7. Melchizedek in Inter-Testamental Literature

2.7.1 Qumran Expectations: 11QMelchizedek and Priestly Messiah

The Qumran community's fragmentary scroll 11QMelchizedek expands Melchizedek's role into an eschatological deliverer who enacts God's vengeance and frees captives at the end of days, reflecting deep sectarian hopes for cosmic rectification. The text equates Melchizedek with the "Angel of Justice," using language from Isaiah 61:2 and Daniel 7 to portray him as a heavenly being who will judge the wicked and atone for the righteous community. The scroll's context—amid rigorous purity laws and apocalyptic dualism—suggests a longing for a priest-king who transcends flawed earthly institutions and establishes God's reign unchallenged. This Qumran interpretation portrays Melchizedek as prefiguring a Messiah who combines sacrificial atonement with judicial authority, embodying both priestly and royal functions. The unity of these roles conforms to the community's expectation that ultimate deliverance would involve both spiritual redemption and political vindication. Understanding these Qumranic anticipations helps us see how Second-Temple Jews read Genesis 14's brief episode as a promise of a world-transforming figure—an expectation later appropriated and reinterpreted by early Christians in light of Christ's life, death, and exaltation.

2.7.2 2 Enoch and the Heavenly Liturgy

The Slavonic text of 2 Enoch offers a visionary account of Melchizedek's heavenly ministry, depicting him ministering before God's throne amidst angelic hosts. In this narrative, Enoch ascends through celestial realms and observes Melchizedek clothed in radiant garments, leading numerous angels in sacrificial worship and thanksgiving. The text emphasizes his unbroken tenure, serving continuously without cessation, and portrays his liturgy as the archetype for all earthly worship. 2 Enoch's portrayal thus reinforces the notion that true priesthood originates in the heavens, not on earth, and that Melchizedek's ministry serves as a bridge between divine and human liturgies. This extrabiblical tradition enriches our understanding of how Jewish mysticism conceived of Melchizedek as a perpetual heavenly high priest whose worship patterns set the standard for Israel's and the church's ceremonies. By transitioning from Qumran's apocalyptic warrior to 2 Enoch's cosmic worship leader, we perceive the breadth of Jewish imagination concerning priest-kings, illustrating that early communities sought a figure who combined cultic expertise with eschatological authority.

2.7.3 Allusions in Philo and Josephus

Philo of Alexandria, the Hellenistic Jewish philosopher, treats Melchizedek allegorically, seeing him as a personification of the Logos's work of wisdom and justice, mediating divine virtues to humanity. For Philo, Melchizedek's righteousness epitomizes the soul's alignment with God, while his peace signifies the harmony resulting from philosophical contemplation. By integrating Platonic categories with Jewish exegesis, Philo elevates Melchizedek into a universal archetype of virtuous mediation. Josephus, in his Antiquities, offers a more historical gloss, acknowledging Melchizedek as a king and priest of Salem without delving into theological typology. His account, however, affirms the antiquity and legitimacy of the Canaanite priestly tradition encountered by Abram, underscoring the narrative's deep roots. Together, these Greco-Roman era writers reflect diverse interpretive currents—philosophical, historical, and theological—that shaped Jewish and early Christian perceptions of Melchizedek. As we move into Hebrews' application, we will see how these strands coalesce into a robust Christological reading that surpasses preceding traditions.

2.8. Hebrews 5–7: Typology Realized

2.8.1 Literary Strategy: From Imperfect Copies to Perfect Priest

The Epistle to the Hebrews introduces its typological argument by contrasting the imperfect, shadowy Levitical system with the perfect priesthood of Christ, who serves in a heavenly sanctuary not made with human hands (Hebrews 9:11–12). The author employs rhetorical questions to expose the insufficiency of animal sacrifices, reminding readers that such offerings "can never, by the same sacrifices repeatedly offered, make perfect those who draw near" (Hebrews 10:1). By invoking Melchizedek, whose priesthood predates and supersedes the Law, Hebrews establishes a precedent for a superior covenant mediator. The narrative structure moves from identifying Christ's qualifications—suffering, obedience, and divine appointment—to explicating Melchizedek's typological role as an eternal priest (Hebrews 5:8–10). Detailed exegesis of Genesis 14 and Psalm 110 then unfolds to demonstrate that Jesus fulfills every nuance of the Melchizedekian order. This literary strategy underscores that the Levitical priesthood, while serving its purpose, was always provisional—"a shadow of the good things to come, not the true form of these realities" (Hebrews 10:1). As the author guides readers through scriptural cross-referencing and theological exposition, the crescendo arrives in the declaration that Christ's offering "perfects forever those who are being sanctified" (Hebrews 10:14).

2.8.2 "Without Beginning of Days": Exegetical Focus on Hebrews 7:3

Hebrews 7:3's statement that Melchizedek is "without father or mother or genealogy, having neither beginning of days nor end of life" invites careful examination. The author leans on this silence in Genesis to argue that Melchizedek's priesthood transcends temporal constraints, thus foreshadowing Christ's eternal mediation. By interpreting the lack of recorded ancestry not as ignorance but as theological signifying, Hebrews emphasizes that Jesus, too, belongs to an order whose legitimacy stems from divine oath rather than human genealogy (Hebrews 7:20–22). The concept of "no beginning of days" resonates with Jewish and Platonic notions of timeless intermediary figures, yet the epistle grounds its meaning in the canonical text to avoid speculative ascent. This exegetical focus serves to demonstrate that the new covenant mediator operates outside the cycle of birth, death, and succession that marks Aaronic priests. This insight elevates readers' understanding of priesthood from a temporal office to a participation in divine eternity, calling believers to trust in an unending intercession that secures their salvation.

2.8.3 Oath versus Law: Covenant Shift and Superiority (Hebrews 7:20–22)

The contrast between priestly appointment by covenant oath and by the Law underscores the new covenant's superiority. Whereas Aaronic priests derive authority from birthright codified in the Mosaic Law (Numbers 3), Christ's priesthood is ratified through God's solemn oath—"The Lord has sworn and will not change his mind, 'You are a priest forever'"—quoted from Psalm 110 (Hebrews 7:21). This oath-based induction signifies a more binding and unchangeable covenant, ensuring that Christ's priesthood cannot be annulled by human failure or death. The author stresses that the Law could not establish this unbreakable guarantee, highlighting the shift from written code to divine promise. This covenantal transformation elevates faith in God's unshakable word above reliance on institutional prescriptions. For New Covenant believers, this means their access to God rests not on human intermediaries but on the inviolable oath establishing Christ's lasting mediation. As we consider the perfection secured by this priesthood next, the superiority of oath over Law emerges as a key theological linchpin.

2.8.4 Perfection through an Indestructible Life

The culmination of Hebrews' typology arrives in the affirmation that Christ holds his priesthood permanently "because he continues forever" (Hebrews 7:24). Unlike mortal priests who die and must be succeeded, Jesus "always lives to make intercession" for the redeemed (Hebrews 7:25). His indestructible life secures complete atonement in a single sacrifice, eliminating the need for ongoing animal offerings (Hebrews 10:10–12). This perfection accomplishes two essential truths: first, that God's requirement for holiness has been fully met in Christ's obedience, and second, that believers now enjoy unbroken access to God's presence. The imagery of Christ as both conqueror of death and eternal high priest resonates with Philippians 2:9–11 and Revelation 1:18, reinforcing the cosmic scope of his intercession. For the early church, this doctrine provided assurance amid persecution, affirming that no power could displace their Mediator. Today, it sustains Christian confidence in the sufficiency of Christ's work, liberating worship from ritual repetition and orienting faith toward the living, active mediator seated at God's right hand.

2.9. Christ's High Priesthood: Substance of the Shadows

2.9.1 Incarnation as Priestly Qualification (Hebrews 2:17)

The incarnation of the Son of God marks the foundational qualification for His high priestly ministry, for only one who fully partakes in human nature can compassionately mediate between God and humanity. In becoming flesh, the Word assumed the frailties and vulnerabilities of human existence—hunger, sorrow, temptation—yet without sin, thus identifying perfectly with those He saves. Hebrews 2:17 underscores this necessity: Christ "had to be made like his brothers in every respect, so that he might become a merciful and faithful high priest." His birth in a human womb and life among men validate His capacity to bridge the chasm wrought by sin. Unlike the Aaronic priests, who represented God to Israel but remained fundamentally separate, Jesus stands among us as true God and true man. His human lineage—through Mary—does not negate His divine preexistence but demonstrates His solemn entry into our condition. This confluence of natures ensures that when He offers Himself as a sacrifice, it is both fully human and fully divine, carrying infinite worth. The incarnation thus elevates priesthood beyond a hereditary function into a redemptive act: God Himself enters the world to restore fellowship. Recognizing this qualification prepares us to appreciate the once-for-all sacrifice He would make and the continuing efficacy of His priesthood.

2.9.2 Once-for-All Sacrifice and the Veil Torn (Hebrews 10:10–20)

The heart of Christ's priesthood resides in His single, all-sufficient sacrifice, which renders repeated animal offerings obsolete. Hebrews 10:10–14 contrasts the perpetual insufficiency of Levitical sacrifices—"they can never make perfect those who draw near"—with the efficacy of Christ's one offering that "perfects forever those who are being sanctified." His death tore the veil in the temple, symbolizing the removal of barriers between God and His people (Matthew 27:51). Where the high priest once entered behind the veil annually, Jesus entered "once for all into the holy places" by His own blood (Hebrews 9:12). This act of once-for-all atonement achieves complete forgiveness, satisfying God's justice and inaugurating access to the Father. Believers now approach the throne of grace with confidence, no longer estranged by sin or limited by ritual prescriptions. The torn veil also signals Christ's victory over death and the demonic powers that held humanity captive. The narrative of successive sacrifices thus gives way to the definitive work accomplished at Calvary, shifting the locus of worship from temple rites to personal faith in the crucified and risen Lord. Understanding this transformation is crucial before considering His ascension and perpetual intercession.

2.9.3 Ascension, Heavenly Session, and Ongoing Intercession (Hebrews 7:25)

Following His resurrection, Christ's ascension to heaven inaugurates His session at the right hand of the Father, where He serves as our perpetual intercessor. Hebrews 7:25 proclaims that, because He lives forever, He "is able to save to the uttermost those who draw near to God through him." His heavenly ministry involves presenting the merits of His atoning work before the throne, ensuring that each confession of sin is met with mercy and each plea for help receives compassionate response. In this role, He functions as both advocate and mediator, sustaining the people of God until the consummation of His kingdom. Unlike mortal priests whose service ceased at death, Jesus's indestructible life secures eternal access, guaranteeing that no believer is ever abandoned. His ongoing intercession also exemplifies the unity of His kingly authority and priestly care—He rules over creation while tenderly tending to individual needs. The imagery of a high priest continually ministering in the heavenly sanctuary shifts worshippers' gaze upward, reminding them of the cosmic dimensions of salvation. This heavenly session sets the stage for a universal priesthood that extends beyond ethnic Israel, pointing toward the church's calling in Christ.

2.9.4 Universal Scope: Jew and Gentile Reconciled

A pivotal aspect of Christ's Melchizedekian priesthood is its universal scope, inviting both Jews and Gentiles into the family of God. Ephesians 2:14–18 affirms that through Christ we "both have access in one Spirit to the Father," breaking down the dividing wall of hostility. This reconciliation fulfills Old Testament promises that exile from God's presence would end and that all nations would stream to the Lord's house

(Isaiah 2:2–3). Christ's priesthood transcends national boundaries, abolishing the exclusive cultic privileges once reserved for Israel's lineage. In His person, the covenant extends blessings to every tribe, tongue, and nation, echoing Melchizedek's ancient service to a foreign patriarch. The multiethnic church thus embodies the global priesthood envisioned in prophetic and apostolic writings. Believers everywhere share in Christ's intercession, offering spiritual sacrifices of praise, service, and witness. As the book of Revelation pictures a great multitude from every nation before the throne (Revelation 7:9–10), we recognize that the high priestly work of Christ draws diverse peoples into one holy priesthood. This universal dimension paves the way for exploring how the Eucharist enacts and sustains Christ's priestly presence among the gathered faithful.

2.10. Eucharistic Resonances: Bread, Wine, and New-Covenant Worship

2.10.1 Last Supper as Melchizedekian Meal (Luke 22:19–20)

On the eve of His crucifixion, Jesus instituted the Lord's Supper using bread and wine, the same elements Melchizedek first placed before Abram. Luke 22:19–20 recounts Jesus taking bread, blessing it, and declaring, "This is my body, which is given for you," and likewise with the cup as "the new covenant in my blood." This sacramental action does more than memorialize; it reorients the elements into a living sign of Christ's once-for-all sacrifice and ongoing priesthood. By blessing the bread and cup, Jesus assumes the role of priest, consecrating the gifts to mediate grace and forgiveness. The New Testament letters encourage believers to partake "in remembrance" of Him, thus participating in His one eternal sacrifice. Unlike Old Testament offerings that repeated, the Eucharist proclaims the singular efficacy of Christ's work while anticipating its consummation. The Last Supper's structure echoes Melchizedek's offering of bread and wine yet transforms it by embedding sacrificial meaning and covenant renewal at the very moment of betrayal and death. Recognizing this connection deepens our appreciation for the Lord's Table as a Melchizedekian meal that binds together remembrance, present grace, and future hope.

2.10.2 Early Christian Liturgy in Acts and the Didache

The earliest Christian communities swiftly embraced a regular pattern of "breaking bread" and prayer, as recorded in Acts 2:42 and 20:7, underscoring the centrality of the Eucharist in worship. The Didache, a late-first- or early-second-century manual, provides liturgical instructions for giving thanks over the cup and the broken bread, reflecting an established ritual resembling Melchizedek's meal rather than Levitical sacrifice. These eucharistic prayers invoke Christ's body and blood, the unity of the church, and the eschatological banquet yet to come. The rituals foster communal solidarity, bind participants into one body by their shared partaking, and proclaim the death of the Lord until He returns. This early liturgy emphasizes both thanksgiving (eucharistia) and anticipation, situating the Eucharist as foretaste of the kingdom. The absence of animal offerings and the direct appeal to Christ's once-for-all offering highlight the transition from shadow to substance. Believers saw in the communal meal a continuation of Melchizedek's ancient act, reinterpreted through the lens of Christ's priesthood. As we turn to sacramental theology, these liturgical practices illustrate how the church embodies priestly worship in every age.

2.10.3 Sacramental Theology: Real Presence and Covenant Renewal

Theological reflection on the Eucharist converges on the doctrine of Christ's real presence and the renewal of covenant relationships. Various traditions articulate this presence differently—ranging from substantial presence in the elements to spiritual reception by faith—yet all affirm that Christ is uniquely operative in the sacrament. The Eucharist signifies the covenant renewal prophesied in Jeremiah 31:31–34, where God declares He will write His law on human hearts. When participants receive the bread and cup, they enact the new covenant, affirming forgiveness of sins and empowerment for righteous living. Augustine's view of sacramental participation as "food of immortality" echoes Melchizedek's bread and wine offering as nourishment for covenant life. Reformed theology emphasizes the spiritual feeding on Christ by faith, locating the sacrament's power in the Spirit's work rather than in the elements themselves. Liturgical scholars note that the pattern of Word and sacrament together fulfills the priestly proclamation of God's word and the enactment of His promises. This sacramental theology anchors Christian worship in a Melchizedekian paradigm—where simple gifts become vessels of divine grace, bridging heaven and earth until the wedding feast of the Lamb (Revelation 19:9).

2.11. The Priesthood of All Believers

2.11.1 Royal-Priestly Identity in 1 Peter 2:9

In 1 Peter 2:9, the apostle declares believers to be "a chosen race, a royal priesthood, a holy nation, a people for his own possession," language that echoes Exodus 19:6's promise to Israel and Psalm 110's royal-priestly motif. This designation democratizes priesthood, extending mediatorial functions to every believer. By calling us "royal," Peter connects us to the kingly authority of Christ; by "priesthood," he affirms our calling to intercede for others, offer spiritual sacrifices, and proclaim God's excellencies. This dual identity frames Christian vocation as both service and sovereignty—serving one another in love while exercising dominion over sin and darkness through prayer and testimony. The priesthood of all believers affirms that each member can approach God without human intermediaries, yet this privilege carries responsibility to represent God in the world. As we transition to discussing Spirit-enabled ministry, we see that this priesthood is not an abstract status but an active calling empowered by the Spirit's gifts.

2.11.2 Spirit-Enabled Ministry and Spiritual Sacrifices

The outpouring of the Holy Spirit at Pentecost inaugurates the priesthood of all believers by equipping each Christian with gifts for ministry (Acts 2; 1 Corinthians 12). The Spirit empowers believers to pray with insight, intercede for the sick, prophesy, and teach—all acts of priestly mediation. Peter's mention of "spiritual sacrifices" in the same verse underscores that worship extends beyond liturgical acts to include lives offered in holiness, acts of mercy, and ethical witness (Romans 12:1). Every believer thus becomes a living sacrifice, their daily conduct consecrating the name of Christ before neighbors and nations. The communal dimension of Spirit gifts also reflects Melchizedek's offering to Abram: the church's ministries build up the body, nourish faith, and extend blessing. Recognizing this dynamic calls us to embrace our priestly responsibilities while relying wholly on the Spirit's enabling grace.

2.11.3 Ethical and Missional Implications for the Church

The priesthood of all believers carries profound ethical and missional implications. Ethically, Christians are called to embody justice, mercy, and faithfulness in every sphere of life, acting as God's ambassadors and mediating His righteousness (Matthew 5:13–16). Socially, this priesthood breaks down barriers of class, race, and gender, for "there is neither Jew nor Greek" in Christ (Galatians 3:28), fostering inclusive communities that reflect God's heart for all peoples. Missionally, the church proclaims the gospel by word and deed, offering spiritual sacrifices—praise, confession, service—that draw others toward reconciliation with God. The priesthood thus becomes a framework for holistic ministry, integrating evangelism, discipleship, and social action. As we prepare to conclude this chapter, we see that the priesthood of all believers roots Christian identity in Christ's Melchizedekian order, shaping corporate life and witness in anticipation of God's eschatological fulfillment.

Conclusion

Having examined the rise, form, and limits of Israel's priesthood, we recognize how every ritual— from sacrifice to incense, from high-priestly garments to scapegoat ceremonies—served as a dim reflection of the true and lasting mediation to come. The patterns once confined to the wilderness and temple courts now find fulfillment in Christ's once-for-all offering and unending intercession, rendering obsolete the need for repeated animal sacrifices (Hebrews 7:27; Hebrews 10:10–14). This typological progression not only vindicates the ancient rites but also invites believers into a new era of direct access, where faith lays hold of divine reality rather than shadows of it. As our study progresses, the priesthood's shadow will give way to the marriage of kingly and priestly authority in Melchizedek's own person, preparing us to explore how sovereignty and sacrament converge in the eternal reign of God's Anointed.

Chapter 3: Kingship and Sovereignty

When Melchizedek steps onto the stage of Genesis, he is introduced not only as a priest but as the "king of Salem," binding crown and censer in a single hand. That brief description—easily overlooked—plants a seed that will grow into one of Scripture's grandest theological themes: the conviction that all true authority, whether sacred or civic, derives from the sovereignty of God Most High. This chapter traces that royal thread from its earliest appearance in patriarchal days through the Davidic covenant, the prophetic horizon, and finally its fulfilment in Christ's exaltation. By exploring how peace (shalom) and righteousness (ṣedeq) converge in Melchizedek's reign—and how later writers deploy those same motifs for Israel's kings and for the promised Messiah—we gain a clearer vision of the kingdom Christ inaugurates and will ultimately consummate. The goal is not merely historical reconstruction; it is to discern how the theology of kingship shapes the church's public witness, ethical life, and hope for the new creation. With that horizon in view, we now follow the ancient path from Salem's quiet hilltop to Zion's eternal throne.

3.1. Crown and Covenant

3.1.1 Historical-Theological Rationale for Studying Biblical Kingship

The biblical narrative consistently presents kingship as more than a political office—it is a divinely instituted mechanism for reflecting God's sovereign rule on earth. From the early clan leaders in Genesis to the unified monarchy under David, Scripture shows how human authority must bear the imprint of divine justice and mercy. Studying biblical kingship equips readers to discern how Israel's rulers were both products of their cultural milieu and participants in God's redemptive purposes. It also exposes the tensions inherent in combining human ambition with divine mandate, as exemplified by Saul's tragic reign (1 Samuel 13) and Solomon's eventual drift into idolatry (1 Kings 11). Theological reflection on kingship illuminates how Christ's reign transcends all human kings, fulfilling the promises of a "king after God's own heart" (1 Samuel 13:14) in perfect righteousness. Moreover, understanding the covenantal dimensions of ancient monarchies helps the church today frame its own grasp of authority, leadership, and submission under Christ. By tracing the genealogy of kingly concepts—from tribal chieftains to the theocratic rule envisioned in the Mosaic Law—we see that biblical kingship is inseparable from covenant fidelity. This exploration lays the groundwork for appreciating Melchizedek's integrated priest-king office as a precursor to the Messiah's singular rule. Having established why kingship matters theologically, we now turn to the wider ancient context that shaped Near Eastern political theology.

3.1.2 From Tribal Chieftains to Divine Monarchies— Setting the Stage

In the early chapters of Genesis, leadership often took the form of charismatic chieftains who guided family groups in pastoral or military endeavors. Figures like Abraham, Isaac, and Jacob exercised authority over kinship networks but lacked formal coronation rituals. As Israel coalesced into a nation, the demand for centralized authority grew, prompting the transition from judges to monarchy in 1 Samuel 8, where the people explicitly request "a king to judge us like all the nations." This shift marks a watershed moment in salvation history, as divine theocracy gives way to human kingship under divine oversight. The ensuing reigns reveal both the potential and pitfalls: David's victories illustrate God's empowerment of a chosen ruler, while his moral failures underscore the dangers of unchecked power. Solomon's wisdom and wealth contrast with his idolatrous end, demonstrating that human kingship—even at its height— remains provisional. Yet prophetic texts like Isaiah 6 and Jeremiah 23 insist that true divine monarchy will be realized in the "Branch" to come, blending priestly purity with royal justice. Setting this historical stage highlights humanity's longstanding tension: craving a human ruler yet longing for God's perfect reign. With these dynamics in view, we can better appreciate how Melchizedek's solitary kingship in Genesis offers an early glimpse of a sovereignty untainted by human frailty—a pattern the rest of Scripture will gradually unveil.

3.2. Re-Examining the King-Priest Paradigm

3.2.1 Political Theology in the Ancient Near East: Pharaohs, Emperors, City-Kings

Across Egypt, Mesopotamia, and the Anatolian city-states, rulers employed religious symbolism to legitimize their supremacy. Egyptian pharaohs claimed divine sonship, often depicted wearing regalia that aligned them with deities like Horus and Ra. Mesopotamian kings, such as Hammurabi, inaugurated their laws with prologues attributing their authority to patron gods, presenting themselves as earthly vice-regents charged with maintaining cosmic order. City-kings in Canaan built high places and sponsored temple cults to curry divine favor and reinforce social cohesion among disparate tribal groups. In these contexts, the fusion of political power and religious office served practical ends: ensuring loyalty, stabilizing rule, and providing cosmic justification for the ruler's decisions. Yet such systems also bred corruption, as successive dynasties manipulated cultic narratives to extend dynastic claims or legitimize conquest. The biblical writers engage these practices critically, asserting that true kingship recognizes Yahweh's supremacy rather than local deities. When Nebuchadnezzar erects his golden image in Daniel 3, the story pits imperial hubris against uncompromised worship. This wider background shows that Melchizedek's priestly kingship differs fundamentally: he ministers to worship the Most High rather than exploit religion for personal aggrandizement. Having surveyed these political-theological models, we now examine Israel's unique response to this common ancient paradigm.

3.2.2 Melchizedek's Integrated Offices versus Israel's Later Separation (cf. 2 Chronicles 26:16–21)

Melchizedek stands alone in Scripture as both king and priest, a unified office that later Israel would divide between royalty and the Aaronic priesthood. Centuries after Genesis 14, Uzziah's attempt to burn incense in the temple (2 Chronicles 26:16–19) provokes priestly rebuke, illustrating the risks when these offices overlap improperly: leprosy afflicts the king's forehead, a stark warning that boundaries matter. By contrast, Melchizedek's integrated ministry is divinely sanctioned, suggesting that the ideal of a singular priest-king is not only possible but ordained by God Most High. This unity foreshadows the eschatological hopes in Psalm 110 and Zechariah 6, where a future ruler fulfills both roles without overstepping divine parameters. Israel's later separation of offices reflects the community's need for checks and balances, yet it also fragments the holistic model offered by Melchizedek. This separation eventually fosters a vision of a united priest-king, as seen in the prophetic references to a coming Branch who will combine the offices in perfect harmony (Jeremiah 33:15; Zechariah 3:8). Recognizing this tension helps us see why the New Testament returns to Melchizedek's archetype to present Christ's seamless exercise of sovereign priesthood. Transitioning from the tension in Israel's history, we explore how Melchizedek's priestly title amplifies his royal authority in the ancient context.

3.2.3 Why "Priest of God Most High" Enhances Royal Authority

The title "priest of God Most High" confers spiritual legitimacy on Melchizedek's kingship, grounding his authority in divine appointment rather than military might or aristocratic lineage. In proclaiming Abram's victory in the name of El Elyon, Melchizedek asserts that true conquest depends on heavenly mandate, a principle later echoed in David's refrain, "The Lord gives victory to his anointed" (Psalm 20:6). By functioning as God's priest, he embodies the notion that political power must submit to divine prerogative—a radical concept in a world of self-proclaimed gods and deified rulers. This priestly role also equips Melchizedek to channel God's blessing through diplomatic acts like blessing Abram and receiving tithes, effectively creating an economy of divine favor. His dual title communicates that kingship is not merely about territorial control but about stewardship of God's redemptive purposes on earth. In the royal courts of Canaan, where city-kings often adopted foreign gods or syncretistic practices, Melchizedek's exclusive devotion to Yahweh stands out as the model of covenant fidelity. The intertwining of priestly mediation with political governance thus offers a robust vision of authority under God's Most High rule. As we turn to examine Salem itself, the city over which he reigns, the synergy of these offices will become even more apparent.

-

3.3. Salem—City of Peace, Seed of Jerusalem

3.3.1 Geographic and Archaeological Profiles of Early Salem

The identification of Salem with the early site of Jerusalem rests on both linguistic and archaeological grounds. Excavations at Tell es-Sultan, traditionally linked to ancient Salem, reveal fortifications and habitation layers dating to the Middle Bronze Age—roughly the time of Abraham—suggesting a settled community of strategic importance. The city's elevation provided natural defenses, while its position between trade routes connecting Egypt and Mesopotamia rendered it a nexus of cultural exchange. Pottery typologies and architectural fragments unearthed there resonate with contemporaneous Canaanite styles, confirming its role as a regional center rather than a marginal hamlet. Yet no inscriptions have been discovered directly naming Melchizedek, underscoring the scarcity of written records from that period. Biblical memory preserves his reign in a single narrative, elevating him beyond mere local ruler. While archaeological data cannot confirm every detail, it lends plausibility to the presence of an organized polity in ancient Salem. This material backdrop sets the stage for appreciating the theological meaning of "king of Salem" as both a concrete office and a symbol of peace rooted in a real urban context.

3.3.2 "Shalom/Salem" as a Theological Program: Wholeness, Harmony, Flourishing

The root sh-l-m that yields both "shalom" (peace, wholeness) and "Salem" carries rich theological significance. In the Hebrew Bible, shalom encompasses physical well-being, social justice, and divine-human harmony, transcending the mere absence of conflict. Judges 18:6's portrayal of "a land at peace" evokes conditions of flourishing agriculture, secure families, and unthreatened borders. Naming the city Salem thus articulates a vision of holistic flourishing under God most high. Melchizedek's reign over Salem implies that his kingship is defined by cultivating shalom—integrating judicial equity, social welfare, and worshipful communion with Yahweh. Prophetic literature frequently laments the loss of shalom when justice is perverted (Isaiah 59:8), reinforcing that peace is inseparable from righteousness. In keeping with this, Melchizedek's titles of "king of righteousness" and "king of peace" form a conceptual pair that orients readers toward covenantal harmony. Recognizing Salem as a theological program helps us see Jerusalem's later role as Zion, the place where divine shalom will fully dwell (Psalm 122:6). As we move to explore Salem's later theological elaborations in royal psalms, the city's name will continue to reverberate with promise.

3.3.3 Salem in Psalm 76 and Parallels to Zion Theology

Psalm 76 celebrates the Lord's intervention in Judah, describing Zion as "the city of the mighty" and "the city of the Lord" where He breaks the spirit of rulers (Psalm 76:2–3). Though it names Zion rather than Salem, the themes of divine sovereignty and inviolable peace echo Melchizedek's earlier reign over Salem. In both texts, the city stands as a metaphor for God's protective presence, guaranteeing refuge and equilibrium to the faithful. Zion theology amplifies Salem's promise by situating God's throne permanently in Jerusalem, where He will "judge the peoples with equity" (Psalm 98:9). The transition from Salem to Zion reflects Israel's privilege in becoming the chosen location for the temple and the Davidic dynasty. Yet the underlying motif remains the same: God as King who anchors peace in a holy city. This continuity underscores that Melchizedek's brief appearance prefigures the later prominence of Jerusalem as the locus of divine rule. By comparing these texts, we discern a theological trajectory in which Salem's fledgling promise blossoms into the full Zion ideal, anticipating the new Jerusalem of Revelation 21 where shalom reigns eternally.

3.4. Royal Blessing and Covenant Economics (Genesis 14:19–20)

3.4.1 Blessing Abram: Diplomatic Protocol or Divine Prerogative?

When Melchizedek pronounces, "Blessed be Abram by God Most High, Possessor of heaven and earth," he operates on both diplomatic and theological planes. In the ancient Near East, it was customary for a senior ruler or suzerain to bestow blessings or titles upon a vassal leader, thereby recognizing political allegiance and affirming mutual protection pacts. Yet Melchizedek's blessing transcends mere protocol by explicitly invoking El Elyon, thereby situating Abram's achievements within the cosmic scope of divine sovereignty. This act communicates that military success is not an end in itself but a gift from the Most High, who rules over heaven and earth. Abram's receptive posture—accepting the blessing without protest—acknowledges Melchizedek's priestly standing while reaffirming his own covenant relationship. Theologically, the blessing functions as a ratification of Abram's role in God's unfolding plan, mirroring covenant ceremonies like the oath between the parts in Genesis 15. By blending diplomatic formality with divine prerogative, Melchizedek's blessing illustrates how royal authority and priestly mediation collaborate to advance the covenant. This unique interplay sets the stage for examining the economic dimensions of tithing in the next subsection.

3.4.2 The Reciprocity of Tithes—Economic Recognition of Sovereignty

Abram's act of giving Melchizedek a tithe—one tenth of all the spoils—demonstrates an economic acknowledgment of Melchizedek's primacy and God's lordship. In ancient societies, tribute payments signified political subordination and affirmed the recipient's superior status. By voluntarily offering a tithe, Abram recognizes that Melchizedek's authority, and by extension God's sovereignty, undergirds his own success. The tithe also serves as material worship, dedicating a portion of the first fruits to divine service. This practice anticipates the Levitical tithe system codified in Leviticus 27 and Numbers 18, where the tribe of Levi receives tithes to sustain their priestly work. However, Abram's tithe diverges from later regulations by going to a non-Levitical priest, reinforcing Melchizedek's timeless precedence. The reciprocity implied by blessing and tithing creates a covenantal economy in which blessings generate offerings and offerings confirm blessings, weaving spiritual and material realms together. Such dynamics invite reflection on how contemporary stewardship and generosity flow from recognition of God's provision and reign. As we turn to Christological echoes, Abram's tithe points forward to Jesus's affirmation of sacrificial giving and the ultimate Priest-king whose sustenance we seek.

3.4.3 Christological Echoes in the Giving and Receiving of Blessing

The interplay of blessing and tithe in Genesis 14 resonates powerfully in the New Testament's portrayal of Christ as both giver and recipient of worship. In John 6, Jesus identifies Himself as the true bread from heaven, blessing the loaves and feeding thousands, evoking Melchizedek's provision of bread and wine. Likewise, Philippians 2:9–11 describes God's exaltation of Christ, blessing Him with the name above every name, to which every knee will bow—an ultimate reciprocation of divine blessing. The church's Eucharistic thanksgiving mirrors Melchizedek's blessing, as believers invoke God's favor upon the elements and give themselves wholly in response. Moreover, Christ's tentmaking work (Acts 18:3) and reliance on the church's support (Philippians 4:15–18) reflect a form of reciprocal economy, where blessing and offering sustain His ministry. These echoes affirm that the covenant dynamics inaugurated by Melchizedek find their culmination in the Messiah, who perfectly embodies the cycle of giving and receiving. As the chapter moves toward prophetic visions of the coming King-priest, these Christological insights establish how royal sovereignty and covenant generosity coalesce in the Person of the Son.

3.5. David's Throne in Melchizedek's Pattern

3.5.1 The Davidic Covenant and the Eternal Kingdom (2 Samuel 7:11–16)

God's promise to David in 2 Samuel 7:11–16 establishes an enduring royal line, assuring that his offspring will rule perpetually over Israel. The covenant begins with God's declaration that He will make David's name "great" and provide a "place" for Israel's people, signaling stability and divine favor. When God vows that His "steadfast love shall not depart" and that a son of David will "build a house for My name," He intertwines dynastic continuity with temple worship, recalling Melchizedek's union of kingly and priestly spheres. The promise of an eternal throne ("Your house and your kingdom shall be made sure forever before me; your throne shall be established forever," 2 Samuel 7:16) echoes Melchizedek's typological foreshadowing of a ruler whose authority transcends mortality. Jewish interpreters saw in this eternal aspect the coming of a messianic figure who would restore David's reign in perfect righteousness. Christian exegesis appropriates this covenant for Christ, the Son of David, whose priest-king office prevents any succession—He reigns unbroken at the Father's right hand. The covenant's dual focus on temple ("house for My name") and dynasty deepens the link between sovereignty and worship, underscoring that legitimate rule depends on divine sanction and cultic mediation. The promise of an everlasting kingdom also provides Israel hope amid exile and oppression, assuring that God's purposes will not be thwarted by human rebellion. By situating David's throne within Melchizedek's pattern, the narrative prepares us for understanding Christ's universal reign. As we transition to royal psalmody, Psalm 110 will illustrate how Davidic themes merge priestly oaths to anticipate the Messiah's dual office.

3.5.2 Psalm 110 Revisited—Royal Enthronement and Priestly Oath

Psalm 110 portrays the enthronement of a king at God's right hand, a position of honor and judicial authority over enemies (Psalm 110:1–2). The sudden declaration that this king is "a priest forever after the order of Melchizedek" (Psalm 110:4) subverts Israel's norm of separate priestly and royal lines, suggesting a fusion that only the Messiah can fulfill. The oath formula "The Lord has sworn and will not change his mind" underscores the irrevocable nature of this priestly appointment, marking it as superior to Levitical ordination dependent on human genealogy. In the ancient Near Eastern context, oaths by a deity carried supreme weight, binding the divine will irrevocably. The imagery of ruling "in the midst of your enemies" along with the priestly role signals that the messianic king's victory encompasses both military triumph and sacrificial mediation. In subsequent Jewish and Christian thought, Psalm 110 becomes the foremost proof text for Christ's combined office, cited repeatedly in Hebrews (Hebrews 5:6; 7:17). The psalm's spatial language—sitting at God's right hand—evokes both temple imagery (the mercy seat) and cosmic throne room visions (Daniel 7:13–14). By revisiting this royal-priestly oracle, we see how David's dynasty is destined to reach consummation in One who embodies both offices perfectly. As we move to Solomon's reign and temple dedication, the tension between separate offices and their ideal fusion will become even more pronounced.

3.5.3 Solomon, Temple Dedication, and the Ideal of Peaceful Kingship

Solomon's reign inaugurates the zenith of Israel's united monarchy, yet it also exposes the fragility of human kingship. At the temple dedication, Solomon invokes God's presence over the new sanctuary, praying that the place where His Name dwells will be "a house of prayer for all peoples" (1 Kings 8:41–43), reflecting the universal priest-king vision implicit in Melchizedek's title. The peace of his reign (1 Kings

4:24) evokes the Edenic shalom that Salem's name carries, suggesting that Solomon fulfills the monarch's ideal of integrating justice and prosperity. Yet his later compromises with foreign wives and idolatrous practices foreshadow the disintegration that awaits any ruler who departs from covenant fidelity (1 Kings 11:1–11). The temple, an architectural testament to divine presence, stands as a symbol of peaceful kingship when anchored in worship, but its vulnerability to human sin reveals the limitations of earthly power. Prophets like Micah (Micah 4:1–4) later look back to Solomon's era as a type of eschatological peace, when nations "beat their swords into plowshares" under God's reign. This prophetic reinterpretation elevates Solomon's achievements into a hopeful foreshadow of the Messiah's universal peace. As we transition to prophetic visions, the ideal of peaceful kingship embodied and then lost under Solomon serves as a cautionary backdrop, highlighting the necessity of a perfect, unblemished priest-king who will reign eternally.

3.6. Prophetic Visions of the Coming King-Priest

3.6.1 Isaiah's Prince of Peace (Isaiah 9:6–7) and Righteous Branch (Isaiah 11:1–5)

Isaiah presents a dual vision of the messianic leader: first as a child born to us, named "Wonderful Counselor, Mighty God, Everlasting Father, Prince of Peace," whose government "shall have no end" (Isaiah 9:6–7). This title complex conveys divine wisdom, power, and paternal care united in one ruler, resonating with Melchizedek's combined offices of righteousness and peace. The promised increase of justice and righteousness under his reign recalls the ideal Melchizedekic kingship. Isaiah 11 extends the metaphor by identifying the messianic figure as a "shoot from the stump of Jesse," endowed with the Spirit's gifts—wisdom, understanding, counsel, might, knowledge, and fear of the Lord (Isaiah 11:1–2). His reign ushers ecological peace as predators and prey dwell harmoniously (Isaiah 11:6–9), symbolizing comprehensive restoration. These visions amplify Salem's promise and David's covenant by describing a ruler whose authority extends to cosmic reconciliation. The prophetic emphasis on Spirit-anointing parallels New Testament assertions that Christ's enthronement follows His baptism and Spirit descending (Luke 4:18). By articulating moral and social dimensions of the messianic kingdom, Isaiah shapes expectations for a sovereign whose rule enacts both judicial and cultic renewal. As we proceed to Jeremiah, the covenant-faithful branch continues to emerge in diverse prophetic traditions.

3.6.2 Jeremiah's Righteous Shoot (Jeremiah 23:5–6) and Covenant Faithfulness

Jeremiah condemns the false shepherds of Israel before promising a "righteous Branch" from David's line who will execute justice and righteousness in the land (Jeremiah 23:5–6). He portrays this Branch as "The Lord is our righteousness," fusing divine identity and royal office into one Person—an inseparable priest-king theme. This messianic figure reinstates covenant faithfulness, reversing Judah's spiritual decline and ensuring that God's statutes guide his rule. Jeremiah's context of exile and temple destruction intensifies the hope for a ruler whose integrity and knowledge of the Lord surpass the broken leadership of his day. The Branch's ministry restores broken relationships between God and His people, mirroring the holistic shalom envisaged in Salem and Isaiah's visions. By emphasizing covenant fidelity, Jeremiah underscores that true kingship must root itself in God's revealed will rather than human agenda. This prophetic promise resonates with New Testament affirmations of Christ's obedience and fulfillment of Scripture (Matthew 5:17). As we move to Zechariah, the image of a crowned high priest will further articulate how priestly and royal expectations converge in a single eschatological figure.

3.6.3 Zechariah 9 & 6—The Humble King and the Crowning of Joshua

Zechariah 9 forecasts a king coming "humble and mounted on a donkey," whose entry into Zion brings salvation and peace (Zechariah 9:9). The paradox of royal humility subverts expectations of conquering armies, suggesting that the Messiah's sovereignty is demonstrated through servanthood—a motif Christ embodies at His triumphal entry (Matthew 21:5). This image connects with Melchizedek's peaceful reign in Salem, where victory is proclaimed through blessing rather than conquest. In Zechariah 6:12–13, the prophet sees a vision of crowns and a plan for Joshua the high priest to receive a crown, merging priestly and royal symbols in anticipation of the Branch. Though Joshua himself does not fulfill these promises, the crowning vision establishes a template for the Messiah's combined office. The dual focus on a humble, peace-bearing king and a crowned priest reinforces the integrated priest-king paradigm. Zechariah's eschatological temple and restored worship (Zechariah 6:15) demonstrate how sovereign rule and covenant liturgy belong together in God's design. As the Second Temple period dawns, these prophetic motifs inform the messianic expectations that shape Jewish apocalyptic literature—our next topic of exploration.

3.7. Second-Temple Expectations of Regal Sovereignty

3.7.1 Qumran's "Teacher of Righteousness" and the War Scroll's Messianic King

The Qumran community anticipated a "Teacher of Righteousness" who would lead the faithful into covenant fidelity, countering corrupt priesthoods in Jerusalem. This figure bears pastor-king attributes, combining moral instruction with liturgical authority, resembling Melchizedek's union of teaching and blessing. The War Scroll (1QM) describes an apocalyptic conflict where a Davidic warrior-priest leads God's army against the "Kittim," wielding divine judgment (1 QM 1:5–9). These texts portray a messianic leader whose sovereignty emerges through eschatological warfare, cleansing the sanctuary, and reestablishing true worship. The Qumran expectation thus merges judicial and sacerdotal functions, envisioning a ruler who sanctifies the community and enforces divine justice. Such literature expands Melchizedek's brief Genesis appearance into a full-blown messianic scenario, reflecting Second Temple hopes for cosmic restoration. By examining these texts, we see how the integrated priest-king motif became central to sectarian identity and eschatological outlook. The community's rigorous purity codes and apocalyptic zeal underscore their conviction that only a new priest-king could rectify temple corruption and national exile. As we turn to 1 Enoch and 4 Ezra, these apocalyptic thrones and judgments will further elaborate Second Temple sovereignty hopes.

3.7.2 1 Enoch & 4 Ezra—Apocalyptic Thrones and Cosmic Judgment

The Book of 1 Enoch presents visions of heavenly thrones where the "Elect One" sits as judge over the cosmos, dispensing wisdom and meting out retribution to fallen angels and wicked nations (1 Enoch 62–69). This Elect One merges kingly judgment and priestly intercession, as he mediates on behalf of the righteous. The depiction of numerous angelic princely figures serving him evokes Melchizedek's function as priest of the Most High in a heavenly court. Likewise, 4 Ezra portrays a messianic figure—"Son of God"—entrusted with authority to rule and to intercede for Israel's restoration (4 Ezra 13:34–37). These apocalyptic writings envision a cosmic sovereignty where divine judgment and mercy coalesce through a single heavenly agent. While not strictly biblical, they illustrate how Second Temple Jews expanded upon prophetic expectations to develop detailed scenarios of divine governance. Their visions, incorporating angelic hierarchies and cosmic temples, reflect evolving ideas of priest-king mediators who operate beyond earthly constraints. By engaging these works, we appreciate the breadth of Jewish imaginative theology surrounding sovereignty, setting the stage for Philo and Josephus's philosophical and historical reflections.

3.7.3 Philo, Josephus, and the Philosophical Ideal of the God-Given Monarch

Philo of Alexandria interprets Melchizedek allegorically, seeing him as a personification of the Logos's mediation of divine reason to humanity, thus framing kingship as an exercise of philosophical wisdom (On the Cherubim 98–101). For Philo, the ideal monarch rules through virtue and reason, aligning political authority with cosmic order. Josephus, in his Antiquities of the Jews, treats Melchizedek more historically but still affirms his unique priestly office, legitimizing Jewish claims to an ancient, divinely sanctioned priesthood (Antiquities 1.8). Both writers contribute to a Hellenistic discourse that values philosophically informed monarchy—a ruler who embodies justice, wisdom, and harmony. Their works demonstrate how Jewish intellectuals sought to harmonize scriptural traditions with Greco-Roman political theory. The philosophical ideal of the god-given monarch thus becomes a bridge between Melchizedek's biblical example and classical notions of the philosopher-king. This cross-cultural synthesis paves the way for early Christian appropriation of Melchizedek's paradigm in articulating Christ's kingship within a Greco-Roman context. As we transition to the New Testament's presentation of Christ as universal king-priest, we carry forward these Second Temple anticipations into Christian revelation.

3.8. Christ the Universal King-Priest

3.8.1 Inaugurated Kingship in the Gospels: Kingdom Parables and Triumphal Entry (Matthew 21)

In the Gospels, Jesus inaugurates His kingship through parables that depict God's kingdom as a hidden treasure, a mustard seed, and a noble wedding feast (Matthew 13; 22:1–14). These parables emphasize the kingdom's present reality and future consummation, combining judicial themes (invitation and judgment) with celebratory feast imagery—an echo of priestly banquets. His triumphal entry on a donkey into Jerusalem (Matthew 21:1–11) fulfills Zechariah 9:9, signaling a humble yet authoritative kingship grounded in peace rather than military conquest. The crowds' acclamation, "Hosanna to the Son of David," recognizes Jesus as the Davidic Messiah, while the garments and palm branches recall royal investiture ceremonies. Yet Jesus's cleansing of the temple shortly thereafter asserts prophetic-kingly authority to purify worship, linking His royal identity to priestly zeal (John 2:15–17). This royal inauguration seamlessly integrates rulership with temple restoration, foreshadowing His ultimate priestly act on the cross. The Gospels thus present an inaugurated but not yet consummated kingship, inviting disciples to live under His sovereign rule while awaiting its fullness. As we reflect on the paradoxical enthronement at the cross, the inaugurated kingdom reveals itself through sacrificial love rather than coercive power.

3.8.2 The Cross as Paradoxical Enthronement (John 19:19–22)

Pilate's inscription on the cross—"Jesus of Nazareth, King of the Jews" (John 19:19)—serves as unintended proclamation of Christ's true kingship, even amid Roman mockery. The irony of the cross as throne becomes evident: the instrument of shame transforms into the locus of cosmic enthronement, as Jesus reigns over sin and death by His sacrificial death. Hebrews 2:9 confirms this paradox, stating that Jesus suffered death so that through the grace of God He might taste death for everyone, thus securing victory and exaltation. The crucifixion fulfills the royal-priestly pattern by combining sacrificial atonement with the exercise of sovereign authority—subduing hostile powers and opening the way to the Father (Colossians 2:15). The cross's paradox shapes Christian worship and identity: the King is enthroned in humility, and the path to sovereignty passes through obedience unto death. This paradox also resonates with Melchizedek's bread and wine, for Christ's body broken and blood poured out inaugurate the new covenant and manifest His ultimate priestly-kingly act. As we ascend from the cross to the Father's right hand, we will see how His enthronement consummates His reign.

3.8.3 Ascension and Cosmic Session at the Father's Right Hand (Ephesians 1:20–23)

Following the resurrection, Christ's ascension culminates in His session at the Father's right hand, where He "far above all rule and authority and power and dominion" reigns (Ephesians 1:20–22). This cosmic session establishes Him as head over all things for the church, positioning believers under His sovereign care and equipping them to live out kingdom ethics. The Father's gesture of seating the Son signifies the completion of His mediatorial work—He has entered the true sanctuary and intercedes perpetually (Hebrews 4:14–16). Ephesians underscores that this enthronement extends Divine initiative through the church, described as His body and fullness, to manifest His manifold wisdom (Ephesians 3:10). The cosmic scope of Christ's kingship echoes Melchizedek's title "king of righteousness" and "king of peace," for in His session all creation finds its intended harmony under God's rule. Believers thus draw confidence and purpose from His seat of authority, knowing that the King-priest guides history toward consummation. With His universal sovereignty affirmed, the church anticipates the day when He will present the kingdom to the Father, and we will explore that eschatological horizon in Chapter 10.

3.9. The Church as Embassy of the King

3.9.1 Citizens of Heaven, Ambassadors on Earth (Philippians 3:20; 2 Corinthians 5:20)

Christians are declared "citizens of heaven" in Philippians 3:20, identifying their ultimate allegiance with Christ's sovereign reign rather than any earthly polity. This heavenly citizenship confers an ambassadorial role, as Paul describes in 2 Corinthians 5:20, where believers represent Christ's reconciling message to a broken world. An embassy functions both to embody its home nation's values abroad and to communicate its sovereign will to host authorities. Likewise, the church carries the ethos and purposes of the King-Priest into every sphere—social, political, and cultural—bearing witness to God's justice, mercy, and peace. Believers serve as intermediaries between God's kingdom and human society, inviting all to "be reconciled to God." This ambassadorial identity shapes Christian engagement: prayers for rulers, petitions for justice, and testimony to transcend earthly authorities without naïvely retreating from civic responsibilities. The tension inherent in dual citizenship—loyalty to Christ above all yet respect for earthly governments (Romans 13:1–7)—reveals the nuanced stance of an embassy that wields spiritual weapons rather than swords. As ambassadors, Christians embody the kingdom's ethics, modeling reconciliation through forgiveness and sacrificial service. Their dialogue with culture reflects the priorities of Zion theology—shalom, righteousness, and worship—seeking to influence policies and institutions. The church's ambassadorial work thus continues Melchizedek's legacy of representing God Most High to human rulers, carrying divine blessing into every realm. Transitioning from identity to practice, we consider how kingdom ethics shape everyday life.

3.9.2 Kingdom Ethics—Justice, Mercy, and Peacemaking in Public Life

The ethics of God's kingdom derive directly from the character of the King-Priest: justice for the oppressed, mercy for the repentant, and peacemaking as active reconciliation. Prophetic voices like Micah 6:8 crystallize these demands: "to do justice, and to love kindness, and to walk humbly with your God." Jesus amplifies these in the Sermon on the Mount, blessing peacemakers and instructing followers to pursue righteousness that exceeds mere external compliance (Matthew 5:6,9). In public life, justice requires advocating for equitable laws, fair courts, and protection of the vulnerable. Mercy calls for compassion toward refugees, prisoners, and those marginalized by systemic injustice. Peacemaking involves bridging ethnic, economic, and ideological divides, reflecting the shalom that Salem's name embodies. Christian engagement in politics and social reform should flow from these kingdom principles, avoiding coercive power while earnestly seeking the common good. Nonviolence and restorative justice exemplify how peacemakers can transform conflict rather than exacerbate it. Institutions influenced by these ethics—schools, hospitals, charities—become outposts of divine rule. As Christians align public policies with kingdom values, they demonstrate the practical outworking of Melchizedek's priestly mediation of peace. Having explored ethics, we now turn to sacramental signs that anchor allegiance and sustain this mission.

3.9.3 Sacramental Signs of Sovereignty: Baptismal Allegiance and Eucharistic Loyalty

Baptism and the Eucharist function as sacramental signs forging corporate identity and allegiance to the King-Priest. Baptism publicly identifies believers with Christ's death, burial, and resurrection, marking their formal induction into God's royal priesthood (Romans 6:3–4). Emerging from the waters signifies death to the old order and birth into the new creation under Christ's reign. The Eucharist reenacts Melchizedek's ancient offering of bread and wine, as Jesus institutes a new covenant meal proclaiming His sacrificial kingship (Luke 22:19–20). Each communion service renews the church's loyalty, binding participants to the King's body and to one another in covenant solidarity. The sacrament anticipates the eschatological banquet in the kingdom yet to come (Revelation 19:9), reinforcing forward-looking hope. Sacramental participation also empowers ethical living, as communing with the King-Priest equips believers to serve as priests to the world. The visible signs—a white garment at baptism, the broken bread, poured cup—anchor invisible realities of divine sovereignty and priestly presence. These rituals cultivate communal memory of Christ's enthronement and ongoing intercession. As the embassy of heaven, the church's sacramental life both proclaims the kingdom and equips its messengers. Concluding our look at the church's role, we now anticipate the consummation of kingship in glory.

3.10. Eschatological Consummation— King of Kings and Lord of Lords

3.10.1 Revelation 19:11–16—The Rider on the White Horse

In Revelation 19:11–16, John's vision unveils the Messianic King-Priest returning as the "Faithful and True," clothed with a robe dipped in blood and riding a white horse. The imagery evokes both warrior and priest: His eyes like flames of fire symbolize divine judgment, while His name "King of kings and Lord of lords" proclaims universal sovereignty. The blood-dipped robe recalls sacrificial atonement, indicating that His triumph springs from the cross's efficacy. The sharp sword from His mouth exemplifies the priestly word that judges with truth, fulfilling Zechariah's vision of a humble king whose rule establishes justice (Zechariah 9:9). All earth's armies yield to His mandate, and He treads the winepress of divine wrath, executing both covenant loyalty and retributive justice. This eschatological tableau combines priestly and royal functions in a single figure whose authority extends over cosmic forces. Worship of the Lamb in heaven and on earth flows from this consummated kingship. The vision encourages the church to persevere, reminding believers that present sufferings yield to a future of vindication under the King-Priest's direct rule. As this chapter draws to a close, we reflect on how the new creation embodies eternal peace under His unassailable reign.

3.10.2 New Jerusalem: Political Theology of Eternal Peace (Revelation 21:1–4, 22–27)

Revelation 21 portrays the New Jerusalem descending from heaven, "prepared as a bride adorned for her husband," signifying the consummation of covenant intimacy between God and His people. The city requires no temple, for the Lord God and the Lamb are its temple, eliminating any spatial barrier to divine presence (Revelation 21:22). The absence of night and the perpetual radiance of God's glory ensure an environment of unbroken communion. Nations walk by its light, reflecting the city's role as the universal capital where divine sovereignty uniformly governs all peoples. The gates named after the twelve tribes and foundations inscribed with the twelve apostles symbolize the continuity of covenant history culminating in the eschaton. The political theology here advances beyond earthly kingdoms: there are no rulers apart from the King-Priest, for He herself exercises direct governance, dispensing justice, peace, and healing without need for intermediaries. Edenic order is restored—trees of life line the river, and its leaves heal the nations (Revelation 22:2). This consummated polity fulfills Melchizedek's promise of shalom in Salem, now realized on a cosmic scale. As the chapter concludes, the New Jerusalem's vision anchors the church's hope in an eternal kingdom, shaping present witness.

3.10.3 Shared Reign of the Saints and the Restoration of Creation (Revelation 5:10; 22:5)

Revelation 5:10 declares believers "a kingdom and priests to our God," indicating that those redeemed by the Lamb share in His reign and priestly service. This shared reign transcends typological participation, constituting an actual involvement in

Christ's sovereign rule. Revelation 22:5 reinforces this communal kingship: "They will reign forever and ever," affirming the saints' ongoing governance alongside the King-Priest. The restoration of creation—rivers, trees, and the absence of curse—demonstrates that divine authority extends to all facets of existence, renewing cosmos according to covenant design (Genesis 1:28). Human stewardship under Christ's kingship becomes fully realized, as creation's original mandate to cultivate and guard the earth finds its fulfillment in unfallen harmony. The eschatological community thus embodies the dual vocation of priestly worship and royal stewardship, administering God's creational order in a redeemed cosmos. This shared reign underscores the integration of worship and governance first glimpsed in Melchizedek's priest-king pattern. As we stand ready to transition to the next chapter on Melchizedek's mysteries, we carry forward the vision of a people who serve and reign in perfect unity under the eternal King-Priest.

Conclusion

Our journey through the biblical landscape of kingship reveals a consistent pattern: wherever God's covenant advances, sovereignty is re-defined by righteousness, service, and peace. Melchizedek previews this ideal in miniature, David embodies it in promise, and Jesus fulfils it in paradox—enthroned through a cross and crowned at the Father's right hand. Along the way we have seen how ancient city-states, prophetic oracles, and apocalyptic visions all press toward a single confession: the kingdom belongs to the Lord and to His Anointed. For the church, that confession translates into a lived allegiance—expressed in baptismal identity, Eucharistic loyalty, and works of justice that echo the character of the King. Yet even these signs are provisional, pointing beyond the present age to the day when crowns are cast before the Lamb and shalom saturates creation. With the contours of royal sovereignty now fresh in mind, we turn in the next chapter to the deeper mysteries surrounding Melchizedek himself—mysteries that invite still richer contemplation of the priest-king whose order defines eternity.

Chapter 4: The Mysteries of Melchizedek

The figure of Melchizedek occupies a singular place in Scripture: he appears and disappears with scarcely a trace, yet his brief cameo sparks questions that resonate through millennia of theology, mysticism, and art. His missing genealogy, the sudden bestowal of priestly and kingly authority, and the enigmatic bread-and-wine offering compel us to peer beyond the surface narrative into the deep currents of Jewish and Christian thought. This chapter ventures into those undercurrents—examining the deliberate silences of the biblical text, the bold speculations of Second-Temple scrolls, the multiplier voices of the Church Fathers, and even the mystical pathways of Kabbalah. We will weigh the arguments that construe Melchizedek as an angelic intermediary, a Christophany, or a historical Jebusite ruler, and trace how his image has been woven into liturgy, iconography, and interfaith discourse. Our journey does not seek definitive answers to every question—after all, mystery, by its nature, invites humble exploration rather than exhausted explanation—but to equip readers with a panoramic view of how this shadowy priest-king has both challenged and enriched biblical interpretation and devotional longing.

4.1.Veiled Figure, Holy Curiosity

4.1.1 Why Mystery Matters in Biblical Theology

Mystery in biblical theology functions as an invitation rather than a barrier, beckoning readers to trust that divine revelation often surpasses human comprehension. The Scriptures frequently withhold certain details—such as Melchizedek's genealogy—to signal that some truths are meant to be pondered rather than fully dissected. This dynamic nurtures humility, reminding believers that faith involves embracing "things not seen" (Hebrews 11:1) and leaning on God's character rather than exhaustive data. Mystery also protects the transcendent nature of God against reduction to merely human categories; by retaining divine reserve, Scripture prevents theology from becoming mere biography. In the case of Melchizedek, the absence of birth and death records directs attention to his function—priesthood and kingship—over his personal origin. Embracing such mystery fosters worshipful awe, as readers confront a figure who stands as both historical and typological. Moreover, mystery encourages ongoing dialogue between text, tradition, and community reflection, weaving a living tapestry of interpretation rather than a static scholarly footnote. This openness allows Scripture to speak anew in each generation, as fresh questions about identity, office, and covenant arise. Finally, mystery safeguards hope: if every biblical figure were fully explicated, there would be little space for forward-looking expectation. By preserving uncharted depths in Melchizedek's story, the Bible seals within its pages a promise that ultimate revelation waits at the eschaton, when the invisible will be seen (1 Corinthians 13:12).

4.1.2 Methodological Lenses: Canon, History, and Spiritual Discernment

Approaching Melchizedek's mysteries demands a multifaceted methodology combining canonical fidelity, historical-critical awareness, and spiritual discernment.

Canonical study insists we interpret Genesis 14, Psalm 110, and Hebrews 5–7 in conversation with the full witness of Scripture, recognizing how later texts re-read earlier ones. This theological reading guards against eisegesis, ensuring that typologies of priest-king unity align with Christ's presentation. Historical-critical tools probe the ancient Near Eastern context, assessing archaeological data around Salem and comparative cultic practices without reducing Melchizedek solely to a Canaanite potentate. Such historical scrutiny reveals the world out of which the Genesis narrative emerged and the plausible contours of an early city-state polity. Finally, spiritual discernment invites the believing community to seek the Spirit's guidance, as early Christians did in reading Melchizedek as a Christophany. This dimension acknowledges that some aspects of divine purpose may only become clear through prayerful reflection and corporate worship. Together, these lenses form a tripod: the text's internal coherence, its external context, and its living, spiritual impact. Skewing too heavily toward any one risks distortion: strict historicism may overlook typological depth, while purely devotional readings risk anachronism. By integrating all three, we honor the Bible's complexity and prepare to explore the specific mysteries attended by its deliberate silences and bold theological provocations.

4.2. Silence in Scripture: Genealogy Omitted

4.2.1 Narrative Ellipsis as Literary Strategy

 The omission of Melchizedek's parentage and life story in Genesis 14 exemplifies narrative ellipsis, a technique that foregrounds theological import over biographical detail. Such selective storytelling compels readers to focus on the elements the narrator includes—titles, actions, and theological alliances—rather than extraneous data. In ancient historiography, genealogies signaled legitimacy; their absence here signals a transcendent validity rooted in divine appointment. This ellipse therefore functions as a signpost, directing attention to Melchizedek's priest-king function rather than his human origins. By withholding his genealogy, the text subtly parallels the later treatment of Christ's eternal priesthood in Hebrews 7:3, where "without father or mother" underscores unbroken divine mediation. Narrative ellipsis also cultivates intrigue, inviting midrashic and rabbinic expansions that engage with the text's silences. Such expansions, while extra-biblical, testify to the ellipse's power to stimulate theological imagination. Ultimately, this literary strategy reveals the author's purpose: to convey Melchizedek as a timeless archetype rather than a mere mortal figure. As narrative scholars note, ellipses can heighten thematic unity by concentrating on pivotal motifs—here, blessing, peace, and priestly authority. Having considered the function of omission, we now explore how that omission acquires theological weight in New Testament interpretation.

4.2.2 "Without Father or Mother" — Theological Significance (Hebrews 7:3)

 Hebrews 7:3's declaration that Melchizedek is "without father or mother or genealogy, having neither beginning of days nor end of life" elevates narrative silence into doctrinal proclamation. The author of Hebrews reads Genesis's absence of pedigree as typological, teaching that Melchizedek represents an eternal priesthood not bound to human lineage. Theologically, this underscores Christ's qualification: He, too, is inaugurated by divine oath rather than human descent (Hebrews 7:20–22). By emphasizing unbroken priestly service, the text reassures believers of a mediator whose efficacy does not falter with mortality. This eternal dimension aligns with Psalm 110's "priest forever," knitting Old and New Testament strands into a coherent tapestry of divine mediation. Furthermore, the absence of genealogy challenges readers to perceive priesthood as a divine gift rather than an inherited privilege—faith, not bloodline, confers righteousness. This theological move reframes covenant membership: believers are united in Christ's priesthood, transcending ethnic or familial barriers (Galatians 3:28). Theologically, the motif of an endless priesthood also speaks to eschatological hope, where no successor is needed, and the final curtain never falls on Christ's intercession (Hebrews 7:25). Thus, what began as a narrative gap blossoms into a central pillar of New Covenant theology, transforming Melchizedek from historical curiosity into Christological cornerstone.

4.2.3 Early Jewish Midrash on the Missing Lineage

Jewish Midrash and Targumic traditions seized upon Melchizedek's unrecorded ancestry to craft diverse backstories that fill the biblical silence with theological creativity. Some rabbis identified him with Shem, Noah's son, positing that his priesthood predated Abram and carried Noahic righteousness into Canaan. Others imagined Melchizedek as a Gentile convert who learned of the true God from Noah's teachings, thus becoming a living witness to universal monotheism. These midrashic expansions often depict anime-like debates between Melchizedek and idolatrous kings, dramatizing his unwavering loyalty to El Elyon. While not canonical, such traditions demonstrate how the silence in Scripture became fertile soil for communal reflection on lineage, conversion, and covenant universality. The Midrash also explores the implications of Melchizedek's silence: by lacking genealogy, he transcends tribal limitations, embodying a priesthood open to all nations. These stories reinforced Second-Temple Jewish hopes for a new order of worship untethered from ethnic boundaries—a hope that later dovetailed with Christian understandings of Gentile inclusion. Though not accepted in rabbinic halakhah, these narratives reveal the intrinsic human drive to narrativize mystery, illustrating how communities engage textually with divine elusiveness. As we transition to angelic hypotheses, note that midrashic creativity often blends human and heavenly motifs, pointing toward the next category of interpretation.

4.3. Angelic Hypotheses and Heavenly Beings

4.3.1 Angelology in Second-Temple Judaism

Second-Temple Jewish literature developed a robust angelology in which celestial beings mediated God's will, guarded cosmic order, and served as high priests in heaven. Texts like 1 Enoch enumerate angelic hierarchies—archangels, watchers, and cosmic princes—emphasizing their roles in judgment and worship. The concept of an "Angel of the Presence," appearing in Isaiah 63:9, and Michael as "prince" of Israel (Daniel 12:1), reinforced the idea that angels could fulfill functions analogous to priestly and royal offices. Within this framework, some hoped for an angelic Messiah or intermediary who would lead Israel to victory and spiritual renewal. The angelic hypothesis for Melchizedek arises naturally from these developments: perhaps he was a heavenly priest-king temporarily manifest on earth. This view gains traction in communities that saw no strict boundary between earthly and heavenly realms—an idea evident in the Qumran War Scroll's depiction of angelic legionaries. Such angelocentric visions equipped Second-Temple Jews to interpret sparse biblical data through the lens of their rich celestial worldview. As we examine 11QMelchizedek in the next section, we'll see how these angelological currents converge in a portrait of Melchizedek as a cosmic deliverer.

4.3.2 11QMelchizedek: The "Heavenly Deliverer" Scroll

The Dead Sea Scroll 11QMelchizedek (11Q13) reimagines Melchizedek as a divine agent appearing in the "year of vengeance" to atone for the righteous and judge the wicked. The fragmentary text draws on Isaiah 61:2's "year of the Lord's vengeance" and portrays Melchizedek as an angelic warrior-priest who liberates the faithful community. Verses describe him as proclaiming jubilee, freeing prisoners, and distributing salvation—functions blending priestly atonement with kingly deliverance. The scroll's language echoes apocalyptic visions in Daniel and Enoch, situating Melchizedek within heavenly court proceedings. His appearance in a final eschatological drama aligns with Qumran's sectarian self-understanding as the righteous remnant awaiting vindication. Though the text is disjointed, it underscores the community's conviction that Melchizedek transcends mere human status, operating instead as a supernatural intercessor. For scholars, 11QMelchizedek provides rare evidence of early Jewish reception history, showing that even before the Christian era some believed Melchizedek to be more than a Canaanite monarch. This apocalyptic portrait transitions us to the task of distinguishing him from better-known archangels in biblical and pseudepigraphal literature.

4.3.3 Distinguishing Melchizedek from Michael and Other Archangels

Although 11QMelchizedek and other Second-Temple texts portray Melchizedek as an exalted celestial figure, the scroll does not identify him explicitly with Michael, Gabriel, or any named archangel. Michael's role as protector of Israel (Daniel 10:21) and Gabriel's role as heavenly messenger (Luke 1:19) occupy distinct niches in Jewish angelology. Melchizedek's combined titles of king and priest set him apart from these warriors and heralds, suggesting a unique office that defies easy classification. Pseudepigraphal works sometimes conflate major angels with starry-gods or cosmic judges, yet Melchizedek consistently functions as mediator between God and humanity rather than cosmic sentinel. Distinguishing him requires careful analysis of terminology: "Angel" (malak) in Hebrew can mean "messenger," applied both to humans and celestial beings—a flexibility some traditions exploit to blur categories. Yet Melchizedek's narrative role parallels Christ's priesthood rather than Michael's war-bearing. Acknowledging these differences helps guard against allegorizing Melchizedek into a generic angelic office, preserving his typological link to the Messiah. Having traced angelic hypotheses, we now turn to pre-incarnate Christophany theories that see Melchizedek as a visible manifestation of the eternal Word.

4.4. Pre-Incarnate Christophany Theories

4.4.1 Patristic Voices: Irenaeus, Athanasius, and Cyril of Alexandria

Irenaeus of Lyons, writing in the late second century, affirms that Melchizedek prefigures the pre-incarnate Son, arguing that Abram's encounter was a Christophany in which the Logos administered covenant blessings. Athanasius of Alexandria echoes this reading, emphasizing the eternal Son's mediatorial role throughout redemptive history, from Creation to the incarnation, with Melchizedek's priesthood marking a visible instance of divine presence. Cyril of Alexandria further develops the theme, noting that Melchizedek's bread and wine anticipate the Eucharist and point to Christ's sacrificial ministry. These Fathers employ typological exegesis, linking Genesis 14's events to Trinitarian theology and Christology, thus reinforcing the unity of God's revelation. They often appeal to the anonymity of Melchizedek's origins as evidence of a divine rather than human identity. Patristic homilies and commentaries underscore that the early church perceived Christ's ongoing priesthood as foreshadowed in pre-Mosaic figures. This tradition shapes subsequent liturgical applications, as Eastern anaphoras invoke Melchizedek alongside the Lamb when recounting salvation history. The patristic consensus affirms that Christ's eternal priesthood finds its first pledge in Melchizedek's ministry, preparing us for more recent scholarly debates.

4.4.2 Scriptural Arguments for a Christological Reading

Scriptural proponents of a Christophany theory point to key texts: Hebrews 7:3 interprets Genesis's silence on genealogy as signifying eternal priesthood; Psalm 110:4 applies covenant-oath language to a priest forever after Melchizedek's order, cited repeatedly in the New Testament as Christological proof. Theophanic episodes—God appearing as a man without death record, as in Genesis 18's visitation—offer precedent for divine self-revelation in human form. John 8:58's "before Abraham was, I am" echoes this pattern of divine temporality transcending human chronology. Revelation's depiction of the Lamb slain "from the foundation of the world" (Revelation 13:8) similarly suggests that Christ's priestly work existed in God's eternal plan long before the incarnation. Advocates argue that Melchizedek's bread and wine convey covenant initiation rather than mere hospitality, pointing to Christ's institution of the Eucharist as fulfillment. Such scriptural intertextuality underscores the New Testament's hermeneutical approach to Old Testament types. While these arguments rely on theological reading, they maintain fidelity to the text's internal logic and canonical usage.

4.4.3 Modern Critics and Alternative Explanations

Contemporary scholarship offers alternative readings that resist Christophany and angelic identification, favoring historical-critical or literary approaches. Some scholars propose that Melchizedek was simply a local Jebusite ruler whose peculiar portrayal reflects the narrator's theological interests, not divine manifestation. Others argue that the author of Hebrews employs hyperbolic typology, stretching Genesis 14's narrative silence into a theological point without intending literal pre-existence. Feminist and postcolonial critics caution against imposing Christological frameworks on ancient Near Eastern texts, advocating for readings that respect the text's original cultural milieu. Sociolinguistic studies highlight that "without genealogy" might simply reflect lost oral tradition rather than deliberate theological silence. Moreover, comparative mythology points to similar priest-king figures in surrounding cultures, suggesting syncretistic influences in the biblical narrative. These modern critiques invite a measured balance between theological interpretation and historical plausibility, encouraging readers to hold Melchizedek's mysteries with both reverence and critical awareness. As we move beyond these debates to explore historical-monarch hypotheses and mystical reinterpretations, the diversity of voices underscores the enduring fascination and complexity of this ancient figure.

4.5. Historical Monarch: The Jebusite King Proposal

4.5.1 Archaeological Soundings around Early Jerusalem

The identification of Melchizedek with a historical Jebusite king rests on archaeological evidence for a fortified settlement at Tell es-Sultan, often equated with ancient Salem. Excavations have uncovered Middle Bronze II fortification walls and domestic structures dating to approximately 2000 B.C., a period compatible with patriarchal chronology. Pottery assemblages and architectural remains suggest a thriving urban center capable of supporting centralized rule. Epigraphic evidence remains silent—no inscriptions bearing the name Melchizedek have surfaced—but the material culture confirms that a city-state polity existed in the hill country west of the Jordan. Scholars note that the absence of royal genealogies in Genesis may reflect the loss of local archives rather than theological omission. The city's strategic location along trade routes between Egypt and Mesopotamia would have endowed its ruler with both wealth and influence—a plausible context for a king-priest hybrid. Comparative studies highlight parallels with other Canaanite city-states where rulers performed cultic functions in local shrines. This interpretation emphasizes the plausibility of Melchizedek as an actual monarch whose story was preserved in Israelite memory. It invites readers to consider how oral traditions memorialized a powerful figure in the ancient Near East. Yet this historical reconstruction must wrestle with the narrative's theological framing, which attributes cosmic titles absent from typical Jebusite inscriptions. As we balance archaeological plausibility with narrative theology, the Jebusite king proposal prompts us to reflect on the interplay between history and interpretation. This perspective paves the way for exploring the radically different mystical and kabbalistic readings of Melchizedek's identity.

4.5.2 Canaanite Cultic Titles and City-State Governance

 Canaanite rulers often bore titles that combined civic and religious authority, serving as both civic magistrate and chief cultic officiant for local deities. Inscriptional evidence from Ugarit and Ebla reveals kings acting as high priests in temple rituals, performing sacrifices, and maintaining cultic calendars. Such offices reinforced the ruler's legitimacy by linking political power to divine favor. In this light, Melchizedek's dual title as "king and priest" of Salem would have fit within broader regional patterns of sacred monarchy. The narrative's reference to "priest of El Elyon" suggests worship of a high god above the local pantheon, indicating theological distinctiveness even within a Canaanite milieu. This title may reflect a syncretistic development whereby local kings adopted a monotheistic veneer to legitimize their rule over diverse tribes. The Canaanite precedent of sacred kingship offers a plausible backdrop for interpreting Melchizedek's roles without invoking overtly supernatural explanations. Yet Genesis's emphasis on El Elyon and the absence of references to other deities signals a departure from typical polytheistic practice. This literary framing recasts the office not as a mere civic role but as one ordained by the one true God Most High. The combination of historical pattern and theological nuance enriches our understanding of how Covenant theology appropriated and transformed familiar Near Eastern tropes. Recognizing these cultic parallels encourages a balanced reading that honors both historical context and scriptural distinctiveness.

4.5.3 Counter-Arguments: Literary Theology over Bare History

Critics of the Jebusite king proposal argue that Genesis's portrayal of Melchizedek functions primarily as theological narrative rather than historical record. They point out that the brevity of his appearance, the absence of local royal titulary, and the narrative's focus on priestly blessing all serve a typological purpose within the broader covenant storyline. From this perspective, the text deliberately abstracts Melchizedek from human origins to emphasize his typological role as covenant mediator. The argument further notes that if the author intended to record a local king's biography, more genealogical and political details would appear. Instead, the narrative highlights Abram's tithe and Melchizedek's blessing, linking the episode to sacrificial and priestly themes rather than political alliances. This literary-theological approach treats Melchizedek as a symbol of universal priesthood rather than as a historical chieftain. It foregrounds the narrative's function in shaping Israelite identity and expectation rather than providing an ethnographic portrait of ancient Salem. The critique invites readers to regard Genesis 14 as a theological composition engaging covenant motifs, not a chronicle of Jebusite dynastic history. By prioritizing literary theology, interpreters can appreciate Melchizedek's role in foreshadowing the Messiah without depending on fragile archaeological reconstructions. Having explored the historical-monarch angle and its critiques, we transition to examine the rich mystical and kabbalistic interpretations that venture beyond history and theology into the realm of spiritual symbolism.

4.6. Mystical and Kabbalistic Interpretations

4.6.1 Melchizedek in the Zohar and Lurianic Tradition

In the Zohar, the foundational work of medieval Kabbalah, Melchizedek emerges as a central figure associated with the sefirah of Tiferet, which represents harmony, beauty, and the balancing of divine attributes. He is portrayed as an emanation of God's compassion, serving as a conduit through which divine light flows into the world. The Zoharic narrative often depicts Melchizedek presiding over celestial courts, offering bread and wine as spiritual sustenance to righteous souls. His priest-king office becomes a symbol of the macrocosmic balance between justice (Gevurah) and mercy (Chesed). In Lurianic Kabbalah, Isaac Luria expands on these themes by portraying Melchizedek as a participant in tikkun olam (world repair), channeling rectified sparks into creation. He is sometimes equated with an aspect of the Messiah or a precursor to the messianic light that will gather exiled divine sparks. The mystical tradition thus interprets Genesis's elliptical portrait as an invitation to inner transformation, viewing Melchizedek's dual role as an archetype for the soul's integration of judgment and love. This esoteric lens shifts focus from external history to internal spiritual dynamics, encouraging practitioners to meditate on Melchizedek's qualities as keys to divine encounter. As we move to explore sephirotic symbolism, these Kabbalistic motifs underscore the multifaceted layers through which Melchizedek's mystery has been apprehended.

4.6.2 Sephirotic Symbolism: Righteousness and the Crown

Within the Kabbalistic tree of life, Melchizedek's royal epithet "king" aligns him with the sefirah of Malchut, representing sovereign presence and receptivity, while his priestly attribute of righteousness links him to the sefirah of Yesod, the foundation of divine channeling. Yesod mediates the upper sefirot's energies into Malchut, mirroring how Melchizedek bridges transcendent holiness and earthly experience. This sephirotic mapping fosters a rich symbolic resonance: the crown (Keter) represents divine will, cascading through channels of wisdom (Chokhmah) and understanding (Binah) into justice (Gevurah) and mercy (Chesed), all the way to the foundation where Melchizedek stands. His office becomes a living diagram of the process by which divine attributes cohere into a unified praxis of blessing and governance. Kabbalists meditate on these connections to cultivate personal alignment with divine flow, seeking to emulate Melchizedek's integration of opposites. This mystical approach refracts biblical narrative through the prism of cosmic structure, offering a worldview in which human consciousness participates in divine dynamics. It also underscores the universalism implicit in Melchizedek's silent lineage: by transcending tribal boundaries, he embodies the sephirotic principle that divine energy is available to all who align their souls with the hidden flow of grace. As Kabbalistic practice bridges text and experience, the sephirotic symbolism invites a participatory encounter with the priest-king's mystery.

4.6.3 Ethical Implications in Jewish Mystical Practice

In Lurianic circles, the figure of Melchizedek inspires ethical disciplines aimed at restoring harmony in creation. Practitioners engage in specific meditations on divine names associated with Tiferet, cultivating compassion and empathy, mirroring Melchizedek's role as a priest of righteousness. Ethical injunctions—such as kindness to the stranger, tzedakah (charitable giving), and the pursuit of social justice— are framed as acts that mirror the priestly blessings Melchizedek conferred. Kabbalists view moral action as a form of liturgy, each just deed serving as a "bread" and each merciful response a "cup" offered back to the divine. This ethical mysticism teaches that inner transformation and communal restoration go hand-in-hand: as the individual soul refines itself, it contributes to the cosmic tikkun that Melchizedek's archetype represents. The mystical traditions further emphasize the sanctification of everyday life—eating, business exchanges, speech—transforming mundane acts into moments of ritual intercession. These practices underscore that the mysteries of Melchizedek are not academic curiosities but living pathways to holiness, embedding priest-king ethos into the fabric of daily conduct. Having explored mystical and kabbalistic interpretations, we now turn to the vital role Melchizedek has played in shaping Christian liturgy and sacrament.

4.7. Comparative Religion: Melchizedek Beyond the Bible

4.7.1 Qur'anic Echoes and Islamic Exegesis of Mulk and Righteous Rule

Although Melchizedek does not appear by name in the Qur'an, Muslim exegetes have long noted resonances between his titles—"king of righteousness" and "king of peace"—and the Qur'anic concept of *mulk* (sovereignty) combined with *'adl* (justice). Early tafsīr (Qur'anic commentary) by al-Ṭabarī and al-Qurtubī draws parallels between Melchizedek's monotheistic worship of El Elyon and the Islamic affirmation of *tawḥīd* (unified divine oneness). They observe that the offering of bread and wine in Genesis parallels Qur'an 5:93's mention of sacrificial rites, even though Islam prohibits wine, suggesting a broader principle of ritual submission. Some Sufi masters liken Melchizedek's dual office to the spiritual stations of *dhū'l-'arsh* (heirs of the throne) who combine governance with spiritual guidance. The Andalusian mystic Ibn 'Arabi refers to Melchizedek in his impactful work *Futūḥāt al-Makkiyya*, interpreting him as a "Perfect Man" archetype, one who manifests both divine justice and mercy. These Islamic reflections, while not universally held, enrich interfaith dialogue by presenting Melchizedek as a shared locus for discussing legitimate rule under divine authority. The resonance of *mulk* and *'adl* underscores that righteous governance is a cross-cultural religious ideal. By examining these Qur'anic and Sufi perspectives, we broaden our understanding of how Melchizedek's mystery transcends scriptural boundaries, inviting Muslim-Christian conversations on priest-king paradigms. This comparative lens naturally leads us to consider how modern religious movements, such as the Latter-Day Saints, appropriate Melchizedek's legacy in their own priesthood structures.

4.7.2 Melchizedek in Latter-Day Saint Priesthood Structure

The Church of Jesus Christ of Latter-Day Saints (LDS) regards Melchizedek as the earliest exemplar of the higher priesthood, a direct antecedent to their Melchizedek Priesthood. LDS scripture—specifically the Doctrine and Covenants—describes how this priesthood authority "was in the beginning, and, lo, it is in me" (D&C 84:11), implying continuity from Genesis through modern revelation. Melchizedek's combined roles as king and priest provide a model for the LDS understanding of priesthood offices— endowment with authority to minister spiritual blessings and govern church affairs. The LDS temple endowment ritual incorporates Melchizedekic language, portraying Melchizedek as a pivotal figure in the lineage of divine authority restored through Joseph Smith. Mormon doctrinal treatises detail how Melchizedek's priesthood confers gifts of the Spirit, sealing power, and guidance, echoing their emphasis on ongoing revelation and apostolic succession. Mormon scholars argue that Melchizedek's typological function supports their belief in a restored church with priesthood keys identical to those held by ancient prophets. This appropriation, while controversial to other Christian traditions, underscores Melchizedek's ecumenical appeal as a priest-king archetype bridging ancient and modern salvation history. Engaging this LDS perspective challenges us to reflect on how Melchizedek's mystery functions in communities that claim living divine authority. As we examine these diverse faith appropriations, we prepare to explore how New-Age and esoteric movements similarly co-opt his figure for symbolic and spiritual purposes.

4.8. Spiritual Application: Living with Holy Mystery

4.8.1 A Timeless Priesthood and the Believer's Identity

Melchizedek's unbroken priesthood offers a paradigm for Christian identity, reminding believers that their spiritual standing before God does not depend on lineage or merit but on Christ's eternal mediation (Hebrews 7:24–25). Embracing this mystery invites Christians to locate their worth and calling in the timeless work of Jesus rather than transient human achievements. This realization fosters humility and gratitude, as each believer recognizes participation in a priesthood transcending earthly boundaries (1 Peter 2:9). By identifying with Melchizedek's order, Christians affirm that worship, service, and leadership flow from divine appointment, not personal pedigree. Spiritual disciplines—prayer, scripture reading, and sacramental participation—become means of entering this eternal priesthood. Such practices root believers in a reality beyond temporal limitations, shaping daily conduct with a kingdom-minded perspective. The mystery of Melchizedek thus becomes a living reality, informing Christian formation and self-understanding. As identity is anchored in the eternal priesthood, the call to mission and holiness acquires both stability and purpose in an ever-shifting cultural landscape. From here, we extract leadership lessons drawn from Melchizedek's hidden yet potent ministry.

4.8.2 Leadership Lessons from a Hidden King-Priest

Melchizedek's brief but impactful appearance offers rich leadership insights: first, impact does not require longevity—his single encounter reshaped covenant history. Second, authority grounded in divine commission transcends human credentials, teaching leaders to depend on God's calling rather than popularity or status. Third, his servant posture—bringing bread and wine—models hospitality and sacrificial service as hallmarks of spiritual leadership. Fourth, his integration of justice and peace suggests leaders must balance firmness with compassion. Fifth, his anonymity highlights the virtue of servant leadership, where the mission eclipses personal acclaim. These lessons counter contemporary leadership myths that equate authority with visibility. By emulating Melchizedek's discreet yet effective ministry, Christian leaders can foster environments of trust, integrity, and communal flourishing. Organizational structures—church, nonprofit, or business—benefit when leaders prioritize the common good over self-promotion. The mystery of Melchizedek thus becomes a blueprint for leadership that relies on faithfulness to divine purpose rather than human designs. A final insight: hidden work often lays foundations for visible fruit—reassuring servants that their contributions matter even when unseen.

4.8.3 Mystery as Ecumenical Bridge in Christian Worship and Dialogue

The enigmatic figure of Melchizedek provides fertile ground for ecumenical engagement, as diverse Christian traditions share liturgical references, theological reflections, and devotional practices surrounding his order. Eastern and Western churches both invoke his legacy in their Eucharistic prayers, affirming common roots in Genesis and Hebrews. Protestant communities, though differing on sacramental theology, often celebrate his typology in sermons emphasizing Christ's heavenly priesthood. Adventist and Orthodox liturgies feature Melchizedek as a connecting symbol, fostering mutual recognition of one priest-king. Academic dialogues sponsored by bodies like the World Council of Churches have leveraged Melchizedek's shared tradition to explore convergences in ecclesiology and sacrament. His mystery transcends doctrinal divides by pointing to a pre-denominational witness that predates later confessions. The common heritage of Melchizedek's story thus encourages churches to collaborate in mission, social justice, and worship renewal. By focusing on this ancient priest-king figure, Christian dialogue can shift from polemical debates to shared exploration of divine mysteries. This ecumenical potential underscores how theological mysteries can unite believers in communal quest for deeper faith expression. Having considered spiritual application, we now prepare to conclude the chapter with an invitation into the unfathomable.

Conclusion

Having navigated the bewildering tapestry of texts and traditions—from the gleaming manuscripts of Qumran to the soaring frescoes of Ravenna—we emerge with a renewed appreciation for Melchizedek's role as a theological cipher. His elusiveness reminds us that not every divine truth comes packaged in clear genealogies or airtight historical records; sometimes God's deepest messages arrive through lacunae, poetic allusion, and liturgical imagination. Whether we regard him as a precursor of Christ, an eschatological deliverer, or a local monarch whose story invites universal reflection, Melchizedek stands as an enduring testament to the interplay of revelation and mystery. As we move into the exegetical summit of Hebrews in the next chapter, we will see how the New Testament harnesses this mystery—transforming it from an open question into a cornerstone of Christology and covenant theology, and drawing us still closer to the heart of the eternal Priest-King.

Chapter 5: Melchizedek in Hebrews

Among all New-Testament writers, the author of Hebrews ventures furthest into the sacred silence that shrouds Melchizedek. With the skill of a seasoned preacher and the precision of a courtroom advocate, he turns a three-verse cameo from Genesis into the cornerstone of his plea for a weary congregation teetering between faith and retreat. By tracing an unbroken line from Abraham's tithe to Christ's exaltation, Hebrews contends that everything the old covenant hinted at—daily sacrifices, priestly garments, veils and altars—reaches its long-awaited substance in a Priest-King whose life cannot be destroyed. This chapter listens carefully to that homily. It follows the writer's intricate weave of genealogy, oath, and promise; it watches him dismantle the Levitical scaffold in order to reveal the better hope beneath; and it hears the pastoral heartbeat that urges his audience to press on toward maturity. In short, we enter the climactic courtroom where Melchizedek's mystery is finally adjudicated and Christ is declared the definitive High Priest forever.

5.1. A Homily on the Heavenly Priest-King

5.1.1 Occasion and Audience of Hebrews: Persecuted Yet Privileged

The Epistle to the Hebrews addresses a community wrestling with external pressure and internal weariness, compelled to choose between enduring faith and cultural conformity. From the outset, the author presumes readers who already possess deep roots in foundational doctrines ("milk") yet struggle to advance into mature understanding ("solid food") (Heb 5:12). Their context likely included social ostracism, economic hardship, and the lure of syncretistic worship practices, all threatening to erode their confidence in Christ. Against this backdrop, the writer elevates Melchizedek's mysterious appearance as proof that God has always provided a priest-king who bridges heaven and earth. He frames the message not as abstract theology but as urgent exhortation, calling those tempted to revert to old systems to stand firm in the superior covenant. The audience's dual identity—as worshipers of the living God and as subjects under hostile regimes—creates a crucible in which the reality of Christ's high priesthood must be more than doctrinal knowledge; it must become existential security. The author thus crafts his homily to address hearts burdened by doubt, presenting Melchizedek's order as both historic anchor and future hope. By invoking this enigmatic figure, the epistle acknowledges the community's real pains and offers a transcendent remedy. This section's portrait of audience and occasion sets the stage for our exploration of the letter's literary and theological structure.

5.1.2 Purpose Statement: Moving from Elementary Doctrine to Mature Insight (Heb 5:11–14)

In declaring his weariness over his readers' spiritual immaturity, the author of Hebrews signals his primary purpose: to usher them from rudimentary truths into deeper apprehension of Christ's priesthood (Heb 5:11–14). The elementary doctrines he lists—repentance, faith in God, instructions about baptisms, laying on of hands, resurrection of the dead, and eternal judgment—represent indispensable but preliminary steps in any believer's journey. Yet lingering at this stage fosters stagnation, hindering the community from appropriating the fullness of God's revelation in Christ. By contrast, mature insight involves perceiving the subtleties of typology, recognizing Christ's superiority over angels, Moses, and the Aaronic line, and thus drawing near to God with confidence. This trajectory from milk to meat mirrors covenant history: just as Israel graduated from basic law to prophetic vision, so must the church progress from surface rituals to participation in heavenly realities. The writer makes clear that understanding Melchizedek is not an optional curiosity but a necessary milestone in spiritual formation. His purpose statement thus functions as both critique and encouragement—a call to replace slothful hearing with diligent study and active obedience. In doing so, he correlates doctrinal depth with communal perseverance, implying that only through deeper insight can the congregation withstand trials. With this purpose articulated, we turn next to the epistle's carefully crafted literary architecture that supports such theological development.

5.1.3 Methodological Lens: Typology, Midrash, and Rhetorical Exhortation

The author of Hebrews employs a tripartite methodology combining typological reading of Scripture, midrashic expansion of Old Testament narratives, and urgent rhetorical exhortation. Typology underlies his interpretation of Melchizedek, treating Genesis 14 and Psalm 110 as prototypes that find consummate fulfillment in Christ's person and work. He repeatedly quotes Hebrew texts—sometimes with slight variants—to underscore how early Scriptures foreshadow the new covenant (Heb 7:17; 5:6). Midrashic technique surfaces in his imaginative re-reading of Genesis's genealogical silence, transforming it into a theological assertion of an eternal priesthood (Heb 7:3). Rather than a detached academic exercise, these expositions serve persuasive ends: they exhort the community to trust in the superior priest-king and to abandon regressive religious options. Rhetorical devices—questions, contrasts, and sobering warnings—keep readers engaged and self-reflective (e.g., "How can we escape if we neglect so great a salvation?" Heb 2:3). Throughout, the author balances doctrinal depth with pastoral sensitivity, ensuring that complex argumentation never severs from the church's lived reality. This methodological blend equips him to address both the mind and the heart, inviting readers into a faith that is intellectually coherent and spiritually vital. Having established this hermeneutical framework, we now examine how it plays out in the epistle's structural design across chapters 5 to 7.

5.2. Literary Architecture of Hebrews 5 – 7

5.2.1 Inclusion Frame: "High Priest after the Order of Melchizedek" (5:6 ↔ 7:17)

The phrase "You are a priest forever after the order of Melchizedek" braces the pericope like bookends, cited first in Hebrews 5:6 and then affirmed in 7:17. This inclusion frame signals that everything between these verses—warnings, promises, exhortations, and exegesis—serves to vindicate this priestly order. The repetition assures readers that the author's central claim is not a side note but the very thesis of his homily: Christ's priesthood transcends the Aaronic lineage. Within this frame, each argument builds upon the previous, weaving typology (Genesis 14), psalmic citation (Psalm 110), and oath language into a unified tapestry. The structure also mirrors ancient rhetorical patterns wherein key phrases guide audiences through complex discourse. By returning to the Melchizedek formula, the writer renews his congregants' focus, preventing digression into less weighty matters. This framing device thus provides both cohesion and emphasis, clarifying that theological depth concerning Melchizedek's order is indispensable for mature faith. As the narrative arc progresses, readers sense the rising crescendo of argument culminating in chapter 7's grand summation. This inclusion frame underscores the epistle's literary artistry, preparing the way for its chiastic core.

5.2.2 Chiastic Core: Warning–Promise–Fulfilment Movement

Embedded within the inclusion frame is a chiasm that moves from warning about stagnation (5:11 – 6:3) through promise and stability (6:4–20) to exegesis and fulfillment in Christ (7:1–28). The chiastic structure places the dire warning against apostasy opposite the sure hope anchored in Divine oath, creating a mirrored form that highlights the stakes of rejection or acceptance. The outer limbs—warning and fulfillment—demonstrate the peril of remaining at the milk stage and the blessing of advancing to the meat of understanding. At the center lies the oath and Abrahamic example, providing the pivot on which the entire argument turns. This literary arrangement not only enhances memorability but also drives home the pastoral urgency: to waver is to court spiritual failure, whereas to embrace Christ's priesthood secures unshakable hope. Recognizing this chiasm reveals how Hebrews reframes covenant themes in fresh configurations, inviting readers to inhabit the text's rhythmic movement. The chiastic design also foreshadows New Testament authors' broader rhetorical artistry, as seen in Paul's letters and Revelation. Having traced this core, we now consider the transitional hinges that link the warning and exegesis.

5.2.3 Transition Sections (6:4–12 and 6:13–20) as Theological Hinges

Hebrews 6 divides into two contiguous blocks—verses 4–12 and 13–20—that function as transition between initial exhortation and detailed exegesis. The first block (6:4–12) confronts the reality of believers who have tasted heavenly gifts yet risk falling away, employing agricultural metaphor to illustrate the corrosive power of apostasy. The second block

(6:13–20) immediately redirects attention to Biblical precedent—God's oath to Abraham—and to the concept of immutable promise serving as an anchor for the soul. Together, they move readers from fear of failure into the assurance of divine fidelity. This pivot enables a seamless shift into the deeper typological analysis of Melchizedek in chapter 7. The artistry lies in linking moral exhortation with doctrinal confidence: perseverance is not a bare moral imperative but an invitation to dwell in the safety of God's unbreakable word. The transitions thus serve both pastoral and theological functions, buttressing the coming argument with experiential resonance and scriptural authority. Identifying these hinges equips readers to appreciate how Hebrews constructs a persuasive journey—from alertness to stability to illumination. With these structural insights, we turn next to the first substantive exegetical section: Christ's qualifications for priesthood.

5.3. Qualifications for Priesthood Revisited (Hebrews 5:1–10)

5.3.1 Solidarity with Humanity: Compassion Rooted in Shared Weakness (5:2)

Hebrews 5:2 underscores that any high priest must be able "to deal gently with the ignorant and wayward, for he himself is beset with weakness." This qualification emphasizes empathy born from firsthand experience of human frailty. Unlike a detached pontiff, the high priest enters the tabernacle on behalf of sinners, understanding their ignorance and rebellion. This shared weakness does not excuse sin but deepens the priest's capacity to forgive and guide. The author contrasts this with Christ's own experience of temptation and suffering—though sinless, Jesus learned obedience through what He suffered (Heb 5:8). His solidarity with humanity equips Him to deliver perfect compassion without compromising justice. The implication for the original audience is profound: in Christ, they encounter a mediator who both comprehends and redeems their struggles. This theme resonates with Old Testament precedents—Moses interceding for Israel despite his own failings (Ex 32). By foregrounding solidarity, the text assures persecuted believers that their High Priest truly knows their plight and can supply grace in time of need. This qualification sets the stage for examining the source of His appointment in the next subsection.

5.3.2 Divine Appointment versus Self-Assumption (5:4–5)

Verses 4–5 pivot to the critical distinction between self-appointed and God-appointed priesthood. Under the Law, no man takes the honor of priesthood upon himself but is called by God, as Aaron was (Ex 28:1). The author cites Psalm 2:7—"You are my Son; today I have begotten you"—and Psalm 110:4—"You are a priest forever, after the order of Melchizedek"—to demonstrate that Christ's priestly authority originates in an eternal divine decree. This "Today" language echoes the inauguration of a royal-priestly reign at the resurrection, the moment when Christ's sonship and priesthood are publicly affirmed. Unlike human priests limited by lineage and mortality, Christ's priesthood requires no human endorsement; it is a covenant-oath gift. This contrasts sharply with Jewish high priests whose authority depended on genealogy and sacrificial rituals. The epistle's emphasis on divine calling reassures readers that Christ's priesthood is unassailable and accompanied by sovereign legitimacy. By anchoring His office in God's unchangeable word, the text invites believers to rely not on human tradition but on the sure foundation of divine appointment. Having established the source of His authority, we next consider the perfection achieved through His life of obedience.

5.3.3 Jesus' Obedience, Suffering, and Perfecting (5:7–9)

Hebrews 5:7–9 recounts Christ's prayerful submission in Gethsemane, where He "offered up prayers and supplications, with loud cries and tears, to him who was able to save him from death." This vivid portrayal underscores the intensity of His voluntary suffering and His earnest desire to fulfill the Father's will. Though capable of invoking angelic deliverance, Jesus embraced the cup of suffering to secure human salvation. His perfect obedience—learning submission through suffering—culminated in His becoming "the source of eternal salvation to all who obey him." This language elevates Jesus above Aaron, whose first offering resulted in tragedy when his sons disobeyed (Lev 10). Christ's perfecting through suffering contrasts with sacerdotal rituals requiring endless repetition to atone for recurring sins (Heb 10:1–4). His completed work ushers in a new era of direct access and lasting redemption. For believers facing hardship, this precedent offers both a model of faithful endurance and a guarantee of effective salvation. The progression from solidarity through appointment to perfecting establishes a firm foundation as the letter shifts toward exhortation to maturity.

5.4. From Milk to Meat: Exhortation to Maturity (Hebrews 5:11 – 6:3)

5.4.1 Diagnosing Spiritual Sluggishness and Dull Hearing

Hebrews 5:11 opens with an admonition: the author has "much to say, but it is hard to explain because you have become slow to hear." This diagnosis of sluggishness indicates not mere intellectual deficiency but a spiritual resistance to deeper revelation. In first-century ears, "hearing" implied obedience and action, not passive reception. The community's neglect of advanced teaching becomes a barrier to their growth, akin to a body refusing nutritious food. This spiritual apathy may have stemmed from fear of persecution, disillusionment with church leaders, or weariness of legalistic burdens. The result is an arrested development where foundational truths—though vital—no longer suffice to sustain faith. The epistle warns that this stagnation endangers perseverance, for one cannot stand firm on milk alone when the path demands mature discernment. By diagnosing the illness of dull hearing, the writer both confronts and sympathizes, urging self-examination. The metaphor underscores the relational nature of knowledge: it is not about information dumped into passive minds but about dynamic interaction requiring alertness and responsiveness. Recognizing this diagnosis paves the way for outlining the essential doctrines that form the next stage of maturity.

5.4.2 Foundational Doctrines Listed: Repentance, Faith, Washings, Laying-On of Hands, Resurrection, Eternal Judgment

Verses 6:1–2 enumerate the "elementary principles of Christ" that form the basis of Christian initiation: repentance from dead works, faith toward God, instruction about washings, laying-on of hands, resurrection of the dead, and eternal judgment. Each principle represents a milestone on the pilgrimage of faith. Repentance and faith mark conversion's first turn from sin to trust. Washings and the laying-on of hands recall ritual initiations—baptism and ordination—that incorporate believers into covenant community. The hope of resurrection and the reality of final judgment orient the soul toward future consummation. Yet these doctrines, while indispensable, require integration into a broader theological framework. The author implies that mastery of these elements without advancing into understanding Christ's Melchizedekian priesthood is like students reading primer letters but never progressing to literature. The list also reflects continuity with Jewish initiation rites (proselyte baptism, impartation of authority) while pointing toward Christian uniqueness in resurrection hope. This comprehensive yet preliminary catechesis defines the margin beyond which the community must strive. By naming these doctrines, the epistle clarifies that maturity involves not rejection of beginnings but their transcendence into a living, experiential knowledge of Christ. With foundational principles set, the author now calls for active commitment to go on to completeness.

5.4.3 Commitment to "Press On" toward Teleiōsis (Fullness)

Hebrews 6:1–3 concludes the exhortation by urging readers "to go on to maturity"—to press toward *teleiōsis*, the state of reaching Christlikeness. This forward movement implies intentional effort: it is not a passive drift but an active journey requiring perseverance and spiritual discipline. The text implicitly contrasts those who "fall away" (6:6) with those who "press on," suggesting that genuine faith is measured by endurance. Themes of training and exercise in earlier chapters find echo here, framing spiritual growth as analogous to athletic or vocational advancement. This pressing on involves deeper engagement with Scripture, communal worship, and practical obedience, all rooted in the unshakable hope anchored in Christ. The author's tone blends urgency with encouragement, acknowledging the challenges ahead while affirming the community's capacity to advance. By articulating the goal of maturity in terms of participation in Melchizedek's order, the epistle elevates teleiōsis from moral perfection to experiential union with the heavenly Priest-King. This summons sets the stage for the next section's deeper theological guarantees—promises grounded in divine oath—that will support believers in their pressing onward.

5.5. Warning and Assurance (Hebrews 6:4–12)

5.5.1 The Peril of Apostasy: Enlightenment without Perseverance

Believers who have once been enlightened—who have tasted the heavenly gift and shared in the Holy Spirit—face a unique danger if they turn away from faith (Heb 6:4). Their experience of spiritual blessing makes a later rejection more egregious, since they once knew the power of God's word firsthand. This passage warns that falling away after such privilege leaves no path to repentance, for they would be crucifying the Son of God afresh (Heb 6:6). The community, therefore, must recognize that genuine conversion carries with it a demand for endurance. Knowing the truths of the gospel but refusing to live by them amounts to repudiation of Christ's atoning work. The appeal here is not to fear-mongering but to sober realism: spiritual enlightenment must lead to continued obedience. The author underscores that God's grace, once tasted, is not a license for moral laxity but a summons to steadfastness. For readers tempted to abandon their confession under persecution, this stern caution serves as a lifesaving wake-up call. It reminds them that the stakes are eternal, and that apostasy entails irrevocable loss rather than mere temporary setback. Ultimately, the peril is not God's punitive wrath but the self-inflicted exile from the only source of salvation.

5.5.2 Agricultural Metaphor: Rain, Fruit, and Thorns

The author employs the image of land receiving rain that produces useful crops, contrasted with land yielding thorns and thistles (Heb 6:7–8). Rain symbolizes divine blessing—doctrines received, spiritual gifts bestowed—meant to nourish faith. When that same land produces fruit, it fulfills its purpose, providing sustenance and reflecting the farmer's care. Conversely, land that yields worthless thorns and thistles experiences judgement: it is "near a curse," and its end is to be burned. The metaphor vividly illustrates how privileged believers can either embody the gospel's life-giving power or betray it by producing harmful results. Just as agricultural harvest requires patient tending and proper soil, spiritual maturity demands disciplined engagement with truth and obedience. The land's fate depends not merely on rain but on inherent receptivity—faith that yields obedience rather than rebellion. This warning cautions the community that passive reception of doctrine without active fruitfulness leads to condemnation. It also reassures that God's blessings are not deterministic: human response matters. By grounding theological risk in familiar agrarian imagery, the epistle makes its warning both memorable and practical, urging readers to examine the fruit of their faith.

5.5.3 Pastoral Confidence: "Better Things" that Accompany Salvation

Despite the stark warning, the author quickly affirms his confidence in his readers by promising "better things" that accompany salvation (Heb 6:9). These "better things" include the enabling power of the Holy Spirit, the assurance of forgiveness, and the promise of eternal life (Heb 6:10–12). He reminds them that God is just and will not forget their work and love shown in his name. The pastoral heart of the letter shines here: the warning serves not to panic but to prevent collapse, while the confidence anchors hope. The readers' past deeds of service demonstrate that they are capable of genuine fruitfulness. This dual strategy of warning and encouragement reflects skilled shepherding: confronting error while reinforcing identity in Christ. By urging them to imitate those who through faith and patience inherit promises, the author points to a community of exemplars. The reference to Abraham's perseverance (Heb 6:12) foreshadows the next section's focus on divine oath, showing that patient endurance has always been God's pattern. This pastoral confidence thus bridges caution and promise, equipping believers to respond faithfully to the superior priesthood introduced in chapter 7.

5.6. Oath, Promise, and Hope Anchored (Hebrews 6:13–20)

5.6.1 Abraham's Example: Divine Oath

To reinforce assurance, the writer appeals to Abraham's story, where God swore an oath by Himself to bless Abraham's offspring (Heb 6:13–14). Unlike human witnesses who swear by higher powers, God swears by His own name—an eternal commitment that cannot be revoked. This example underscores the inviolability of divine promise: if God's word to Abraham remained unbroken despite centuries of waiting, how much more secure is the new covenant anchored in Christ? The narrator emphasizes that God's two immutable things—promise and oath—provide a firm foundation for hope

(Heb 6:17–18). By drawing on patriarchal history, the author connects his first-century readers to Israel's ancestral faith, demonstrating continuity in God's saving purpose. This rhetorical move transforms Abraham's wilderness pause into a paradigm for Christian endurance. The weight of a divine self-swearing surpasses any tempered human pledge, reassuring believers that their forward gaze is steadied by unchanging covenant love. Abraham's example also models how trust in God's promises fuels perseverance amid uncertainty. This section thus transitions seamlessly into exploring the nature of hope as the believer's anchor.

5.6.2 Two Immutable Things: Promise and Oath

Hebrews stresses that both God's promise and oath are immutable—unchangeable and eternal (Heb 6:17–18). The promise refers to the blessings spoken to Abraham, while the oath refers to God's solemn swearing by Himself. Together, they constitute a double guarantee that transcends any human institution. The oath functions like a legal affirmation that cements the promise in cosmic court, leaving no room for dispute. It reveals that God's commitment is grounded in His own unchangeable nature rather than shifting circumstances or human faithfulness. For a community vulnerable to persecution, this double safeguard offers unshakeable security. The author contrasts these divine assurances with earthly covenants that hinge on fallible parties. In presenting promise and oath as God's two immutables, the writer portrays the believer's hope not as wishful thinking but as a confident expectation grounded in divine fidelity. This doctrinal pivot helps readers internalize that their perseverance rests on rock, not sand. As we turn to the next subsection, we see how this hope functions practically as an anchor for the soul.

5.6.3 Hope as Anchor and Forerunner: Christ Entering behind the Veil

Hebrews 6:19–20 presents hope as "an anchor for the soul, firm and secure," which enters "the inner shrine behind the curtain" where Jesus has gone as a forerunner. The metaphor of an anchor conveys stability amid storms—hope keeps the believer steadfast during trials. The image of Christ as forerunner evokes the high priest entering the Most Holy Place once a year; Jesus' entry into heaven's sanctuary inaugurates a new era of access (Heb 9:11–12). His entry behind the veil—symbolic of His atoning work—assures us that He secures for us an eternal covenant. By invoking temple imagery, the text underscores that Christian hope is not abstract but rooted in Jesus' accomplished redemptive act. This living hope sustains the community's identity as those who dwell before God's throne. The forerunner motif also implies that Christ has paved the way for all believers to follow into God's presence with confidence. By anchoring the soul, this hope transforms future expectation into present courage, encouraging the persecuted to persevere in faith. The certainty of Jesus' continued ministry behind the veil undergirds every exhortation that follows.

5.7. Exegesis of Hebrews 7

5.7.1 Verses 1–3 — Melchizedek Profiled

Hebrews 7 opens with a vivid summary of Melchizedek's biblical portrait: "king of Salem" and "priest of God Most High" (Heb 7:1). This double title highlights his unique office, blending civic and cultic authority in one figure. The author draws on the Genesis 14 narrative, noting Abram's tithe and Melchizedek's blessing—acts that signal reverence and recognition of a superior priest-king. Verse 3 emphasizes his lack of recorded genealogy and his timelessness, asserting that he resembles the Son of God, remaining a priest perpetually. This portrayal turns narrative silence into doctrinal substance, asserting that Melchizedek's unbroken priesthood prefigures Christ's eternal intercession. The attention to semantic details—Salem as "peace" and El Elyon as "Most High"—underscores thematic continuity with Psalm 110. By profiling Melchizedek in this way, the writer establishes the typological foundation for the superior order of Christ's priesthood. This careful exegetical work sets the stage for contrasting Melchizedek with the Levitical line in the next section.

5.7.2 Verses 4–10 — Superiority to Levi

The epistle then argues that Melchizedek's priesthood is superior to Levi's because Abraham, the patriarch of Levi, paid tithes to Melchizedek (Heb 7:4–9). Even though Levi was not yet born, he "paid tithes" through his ancestor, implying subordination to Melchizedek's order. This logic asserts that the recognition of Melchizedek's priesthood predates and outweighs Levitical legitimacy. The discussion of tithing also ties into covenant economics: Abraham's voluntary offering elevates Melchizedek above the mandatory tithe system later instituted under Moses. The writer emphasizes that those under the Law are still "in the loins" of Abraham, connecting Levitical identity directly to the patriarch's encounter. Through this argument, the author demonstrates that the Levitical priesthood, while valid in its time, occupies a lower rung on the divine ladder than Melchizedek's eternal order. The passage thus reinforces the necessity of a new priesthood to fulfill covenant promises. The superiority of Melchizedek's priesthood over Levi's paves the way for introducing Christ as the ultimate high priest in the ensuing verses.

5.7.3 Verses 11–19 — Necessity of a New Priesthood

Having established Melchizedek's precedence, Hebrews 7:11–19 explains that perfection through the Levitical priesthood cannot be achieved, necessitating a change of priesthood (and thus a change of law). The text argues that if perfection could have been attained under the old system, there would have been no need to anticipate another priest, "after the order of Melchizedek" (Heb 7:11–12). The contrast between oath-based appointment and hereditary succession highlights the insufficiency of a lineage-bound office. The legal requirement of physical descent under the Law stands in tension with the divine oath promising an indestructible priest. Verse 19 portrays the Law as a "regulation for the body" and a "shadow of the good things to come," pointing ahead to the substance embodied in Christ. This pivotal argument reframes the Mosaic covenant's cultic framework as provisional, designed to direct expectation toward the superior covenant inaugurated by Melchizedek's order. It underscores that the essence of priesthood lies not in ancestry or ceremony but in divine promise packaged in oath. Transitioning from problem to solution, the letter moves next to the unassailable guarantee of Christ's everlasting priesthood.

5.7.4 Verses 20–25 — Oath-Guaranteed Permanence

Verses 20–25 focus on the divine oath that secures Melchizedek's priesthood and, by typology, Christ's. The citation of Psalm 110:4—"The Lord has sworn and will not change his mind, 'You are a priest forever'"—serves as the definitive divine decree. This oath contrasts with the Law's reliance on genealogical succession, presenting an unbreakable guarantee. The author explains that because Jesus lives forever, He holds His priesthood permanently and "is able to save to the uttermost" those who approach God through Him (Heb 7:25). This assurance emphasizes the efficacy and endurance of Christ's intercession, unlike mortal priests whose service ends with death. The permanence underscored here provides pastoral comfort for believers facing trials, assuring them that their Mediator remains ever active. The oath also reveals the Father's unchanging purpose, aligning with the hope anchored in divine promise. Having laid this foundation of permanence, the epistle now turns to the fitting character of the high priest.

5.7.5 Verses 26–28 — Fitting High Priest Described

In the final verses of chapter 7, the author describes the ideal high priest: holy, innocent, undefiled, separated from sinners, and exalted above the heavens (Heb 7:26). This portrait contrasts sharply with Aaronic priests who, though consecrated, remained sinners in need of sacrifice. The high priest of Melchizedek's order must offer sacrifices for his own sins, but Christ, "having offered for all time a single sacrifice for sins," sat down at God's right hand (Heb 7:27). This decisive language signals the once-for-all nature of Christ's atonement, eliminating the need for daily offerings. The epistle concludes that Jesus was designated by God "a high priest after the order of Melchizedek" (Heb 7:28), reinforcing the chapter's thesis. The detailed character sketch coupled with the contrast between repeated animal sacrifices and Christ's singular self-offering underscores the superiority of the new covenant. This culmination bridges the theological exposition with practical ramifications, as the community is now equipped to trust fully in Christ's priestly work. We now turn to explore these ramifications in terms of Christological and soteriological implications.

5.8. Christological and Soteriological Implications

5.8.1 Perfection (Teleiōsis) Achieved: Access to God Now Open

Hebrews 7–10 develops the concept of *teleiōsis*, orÂ perfection, achieved through Christ's priesthood, enabling direct access to God. The once-for-all high priesthood inaugurates a new covenant in which believers can approach the throne of grace with confidence (Heb 4:16; 10:19–22). This access removes the barrier of sin that once separated humanity from God, fulfilling the promise of intimate communion foreseen in Eden. Christ's perfection of His priestly role contrasts with human priests whose imperfection required repeated sacrifices. The perfection here encompasses moral, ritual, and relational dimensions—Christ embodies sinlessness, offers a definitive sacrifice, and intercedes perpetually. Consequently, believers experience both forensic justification and ongoing fellowship. The epistle thus presents a radical reorientation: worship is no longer mediated by spatial temples, but by a living Person seated at God's right hand. The *teleiōsis* accomplished by Christ anticipates the consummate gathering of the faithful in the new creation, where no further temple or sacrifices are needed (Rev 21:22–23). This perfected access underpins

Christian spirituality, encouraging believers to maintain boldness in prayer and worship.

5.8.2 Once-for-All Atonement: Culmination of Sacrificial Economy

Christ's offering "for all time a single sacrifice for sins" (Heb 7:27) represents the apex of the biblical sacrificial system, rendering obsolete the repetitive animal offerings of the old covenant. This once-for-all atonement satisfies divine justice fully, obliterating the need for further propitiation. Hebrews 9:12 affirms that Jesus entered the heavenly sanctuary not with animal blood but "with his own blood, thus securing an eternal redemption." The epistle contrasts the inefficacy of sacrifices that "can never take away sins" with the efficacious self-offering of Christ (Heb 10:1–4, 10–14). This theological center recalibrates Christian understanding of sin, grace, and redemption. The once-for-all nature of the atonement liberates believers from ritual-based assurance, directing faith to rely on Christ's completed work. It also reframes the Eucharist: no longer a repetition of sacrifice, but a proclamation of the singular, supreme sacrifice. This culminated economy secures believers' standing before God and empowers them for ethical living, free from the fear of mercy running dry.

5.8.3 Eternal Intercession: Pastoral Assurance for the Beleaguered Church

Hebrews 7:25 underscores that Christ "always lives to make intercession" for those who draw near to God through Him, providing unending pastoral care. This eternal intercession distinguishes Christ's priesthood from mortal priests whose ministry ceases at death. For a community beset by trials, the assurance of continuous advocacy before the Father offers comfort and motivation to persevere. The concept of Christ as our advocate (1 John 2:1) parallels Old Testament themes of intercessory prayer but transposes them into an eternal dimension. Christ's indestructible life, guaranteed by the divine oath, ensures that no believer is ever abandoned. This intercessory ministry bridges present sufferings and future glory, supporting believers in spiritual warfare. It also models a priesthood of empathy and compassion, encouraging the church to intercede for one another. In sum, Christ's eternal intercession embodies the convergence of cosmic sovereignty and tender pastoral care, bringing the Melchizedek typology to vibrant, life-transforming fruition.

5.9. Hermeneutical Method in Hebrews

5.9.1 Typology versus Allegory: How Hebrews Reads Genesis and Psalms

Hebrews interprets Old Testament passages through typology, seeing events, persons, or institutions as foreshadows of Christ's reality rather than through allegory, which treats every detail as hidden symbolism. This typological method maintains historical anchors— Melchizedek really appears in Genesis 14 and Psalm 110 was genuinely composed by David—while asserting that their fullest meaning unfolds in Christ's priesthood. The author avoids the fanciful liberties of Hellenistic allegoresis, instead grounding his argument in direct scriptural citations that the original audience would recognize. For instance, when he cites Psalm 110:4 ("You are a priest forever after the order of Melchizedek"), he treats that oracle as a divine decree predicting Christ's dual office rather than extracting personal moral lessons. Typology in Hebrews emphasizes continuity and fulfillment: the old covenant's shadows reach their end in Jesus (Heb 10:1). By contrast, allegory would obscure historical referents, but Hebrews insists on real historical events and personages as God's inspired foreshadowing. This approach allows the writer to assert that Melchizedek's priesthood, though briefly noted centuries earlier, gains ultimate significance in Christ. The typological lens also respects genre boundaries, treating narrative, poetry, and prophecy according to their own rules while highlighting their interconnections. Such disciplined reading reinforces the authority of both Testaments, guiding readers to see Scripture as a unified whole. Having clarified typology's role, we turn to the midrashic techniques that frame Hebrews' expansions on Genesis and Psalms.

5.9.2 Use of Midrashic String-Citations and Stichic Argumentation

Hebrews frequently employs string-citations—a midrashic practice of weaving together multiple scriptural verses to build a single argument. By linking Psalm 2:7 ("You are my Son") with Psalm 110:4, the author constructs a composite proof text demonstrating Christ's divine sonship and eternal priesthood. This stichic argumentation mirrors rabbinic exegesis, where verses are arranged line by line to reveal layered meanings. The epistle's author treats these citations not as isolated proof texts but as strands in a theological tapestry, each reinforcing the other's implications. This technique deepens the rhetorical impact, presenting Old Testament testimony as a cohesive witness to Christ's identity. The approach also signals to Jewish-Christian readers that Hebrews participates in their interpretive tradition, offering continuity amid emerging Gentile expressions of faith. Unlike mere proof-texting, the midrashic method invites exploration of how each text amplifies and clarifies the others. This layered exposition underscores the unity of God's redemptive plan from Genesis through the Psalms to the New Covenant. By employing string-citations, Hebrews both honors and transcends its Jewish heritage, forging a hermeneutical bridge to Gentile believers. As we consider these methods, we next examine the role of the Spirit-inspired exposition that guides this interpretive enterprise.

5.9.3 The Role of Inspired Exposition (*pneumatikos hermēneia*)

The author of Hebrews asserts a *pneumatikos hermēneia*, a Spirit-guided interpretation, in which the Holy Spirit illuminates the meaning of Scripture beyond its surface sense. Early Christians believed that prophetic utterances carried deeper layers, accessible only through the Spirit's anointing (1 Cor 2:10–13). Hebrews operates on this principle, presenting its typological and midrashic reflections as not mere human invention but as divinely authorized exegesis. This claim bolsters the epistle's authority, positioning its argument as a continuation of God's self-revelation rather than a private theological speculation. The notion of Spirit-inspired exposition also shaped the church's reception of Hebrews, granting it weight alongside apostolic letters. By emphasizing the Spirit's role, the author cautions against reading Scripture solely through human reason or tradition, instead urging readers to seek divine illumination through prayerful engagement. This dynamic hermeneutic fosters a living conversation between text and community, where Scripture's depths are gradually disclosed in worship and study. As the epistle unfolds Melchizedek's mystery, believers are invited into an ongoing experience of revelation that transcends academic boundaries. Having explored Hebrews' interpretive methods, we now turn to its dialogue with Second-Temple sources that illuminate and contrast its theology.

5.10. Dialogue with Second-Temple Sources

5.10.1 Comparing Hebrews 7 with 11QMelchizedek's Apocalyptic Profile

The Qumran scroll 11QMelchizedek portrays Melchizedek as an angelic deliverer who enacts God's vengeance and proclaims jubilee, a cosmic role that exceeds the earthly king-priest of Genesis. Hebrews 7, by contrast, focuses on Melchizedek's typological significance for Christ's eternal priesthood, deliberately eschewing apocalyptic warfare motifs. Though both texts elevate Melchizedek above Israel's cultic structures, Hebrews roots its interpretation in canonical quotations rather than sectarian expansions. The scroll's emphasis on Melchizedek's role in final judgment contrasts with Hebrews' pastoral aim to secure believers' hope and access to God's presence. By comparing these treatments, readers gain insight into the diversity of Jewish thought regarding Melchizedek—ranging from cosmic warrior to covenant mediator. Hebrews engages this tradition selectively, affirming Melchizedek's timeless priesthood without adopting the Qumran community's dual-messiah schema. This measured engagement reflects the author's concern to present a universal gospel rather than a sectarian roadmap to eschatological triumph. The comparison highlights Hebrews' canonical fidelity and its priority on Christ's once-for-all sacrifice. As we move to examine alternative Jewish expectations, we discern how Hebrews differentiates its own Christology from parallel Jewish discourses.

5.10.2 Contrasting Qumran's Dual-Messiah Expectation with Hebrews' Single Priest-King

Qumran writings often anticipate two messianic figures: a priestly Teacher of Righteousness and a royal Davidic Messiah who will lead in battle. This dual-messiah expectation reflects the community's desire for both spiritual purity and political deliverance. Hebrews, by contrast, presents a single Messiah who fulfills both offices—priest and king—thus unifying functions that others separated. By interpreting Psalm 110's royal-priestly oracle in reference to Christ alone, the epistle rejects the need for separate messianic agents. This consolidation underscores the superiority of Christ's person and work over segmented expectations. The contrast demonstrates how Hebrews integrates divergent Jewish hopes into a cohesive Christological vision: one Mediator reconciles God and man completely. The single-Messiah model also aligns with the epistle's emphasis on covenant unity and finality. In choosing to affirm one priest-king, Hebrews positions itself as a corrective to dualistic messianic constructs, offering a more streamlined and theologically cohesive resolution. This deliberate contrast reinforces the epistle's theological distinctiveness while engaging the broader Jewish interpretive milieu.

5.10.3 Evaluating Other Jewish Interpretive Trajectories (Philo, Josephus)

Philo of Alexandria, in his allegorical exegesis, treats Melchizedek as a symbol of the Logos's work of wisdom and providence, while Josephus presents him as a historical king-priest without deep theological elaboration. Hebrews diverges from Philo's philosophical allegory by insisting on Melchizedek's typological relevance to Christ's person and work. It likewise refines Josephus's historical notice by infusing it with Christological theology. By engaging these Jewish interpretive trajectories, the epistle demonstrates its capacity to appropriate useful elements—Philo's emphasis on divine mediation and Josephus's historical affirmation—while surpassing them through the revelation of Christ's eternal priesthood. This evaluation highlights the epistle's canonical authority and its role in shaping Christian self-identity distinct from Jewish philosophical and historiographical traditions. Hebrews thus negotiates a space that respects Jewish interpretive efforts without capitulating to their limitations, pointing readers instead toward its revelation of the one Mediator. Having situated Hebrews within Second-Temple debates, we now turn to the pastoral exhortations that flow from its Melchizedekian argument.

5.11. Pastoral Exhortations Flowing from the Melchizedek Argument

5.11.1 Boldness to Enter the Holy Places (Hebrews 10:19–22)

Building on the revelation of Christ's priesthood, Hebrews 10:19–22 exhorts believers to draw near to God with a "true heart" and "full assurance of faith." This boldness arises from the torn veil—Christ's body—granting direct access to the Most Holy Place in heaven. The author urges participants to cleanse their hearts, hold fast to confession, and approach with genuine worship, moving from ritual barriers to relational intimacy. This transition from fear to confidence reorients Christian worship: no longer must priests mediate every visit, for Christ Himself is the faithful High Priest. The passage's hortatory tone encourages corporate assembly, mutual encouragement, and sustained devotion. By framing worship as entering God's presence rather than merely performing religious duties, Hebrews revivifies the Melchizedek paradigm of priestly access. Believers are reminded that their spiritual privilege demands corresponding moral and devotional response. This exhortation thus translates theological insight into concrete worship practice, marking a vital link between doctrine and discipleship. As we move to the next exhortation, the emphasis shifts to the steadfastness of confession.

5.11.2 Holding Fast the Confession without Wavering (Hebrews 10:23)

Verse 23 calls the community to "hold fast the confession of our hope without wavering," emphasizing fidelity to the gospel's core claims. Wavering confession—suspending allegiance under pressure—undermines the assurance built upon Christ's priestly work. The author grounds this exhortation in the unwavering nature of God who promises and provides. Holding fast involves both belief in Christ's identity and proclamation of His lordship in word and deed. The confession includes acknowledgement of Christ's once-for-all sacrifice, His ascension, and eventual return. In a context where pagan practices tempted some believers, maintaining a firm confession reinforced communal identity and anchored ethics. This perseverance in confession mirrors Melchizedek's example of unwavering devotion to the Most High, even amid foreign polities. It also resonates with the martyr testimonies of Hebrew 11, where ancient saints held fast amid exile. By urging unwavering confession, the text bridges Melchizedek's timeless priesthood with present-day resolve, training believers to reflect Christ's steadfast intercession in a fickle world. The call to hold fast naturally leads into the final pastoral charge to stir one another toward love and good works.

5.11.3 Community Vigilance: Stirring One Another to Love and Good Works

Hebrews 10:24–25 extends the pastoral application by encouraging mutual exhortation: "Let us consider how to stir up one another to love and good works, not neglecting to meet together." This corporate vigilance embodies the priestly care of intercession and community oversight. Love and good works serve as the visible fruit of Christ's intercession, demonstrating the efficacy of His priesthood in transforming lives. Regular gatherings—assemblies for worship and encouragement—reinforce spiritual resilience and accountability. The imagery of "stirring up" suggests active engagement rather than passive attendance, highlighting each believer's responsibility in the body. This communal exhortation resonates with Melchizedek's blessing—an act meant to catalyze Abram's covenantal mission. In this way, the epistle ties theological reflection on priesthood to everyday expressions of Christian fellowship and service. The emphasis on not neglecting gathering also counters isolation, which can lead to doctrinal drift and moral compromise. By cultivating a culture of mutual care and proactive support, the church embodies the Melchizedekian ideal of priestly mediation within the community. Having explored these pastoral dimensions, we now prepare to conclude the chapter's exegetical summit.

Conclusion

By the time Hebrews rests its case, Melchizedek is no longer a shadowy monarch from a bygone skirmish but the divinely scripted silhouette into which Jesus steps with flawless fit. The preacher has shown that the very omissions of Genesis—no ancestry, no obituary—were prophetic cues pointing to a priesthood that cannot be revoked by death or replaced by succession. In Christ, the oath God once swore becomes a living guarantee: access to the Father is secure, atonement is complete, and intercession never sleeps. For readers then and now, the argument lifts the weight of ritual anxiety and replaces it with the solid comfort of an unchangeable mediator. Standing on this exegetical summit, the church can breathe the thin air of finished redemption and look outward—toward a worship that is bold, an ethics that is sacrificial, and a mission driven by the certainty that the throne of grace is always open. With Melchizedek's enigma resolved in the exalted Son, the path is clear to explore how that eternal priesthood transforms every dimension of Christian life in the chapters ahead.

Chapter 6: Birth, Life, and (Apparent) Death

Unlike most biblical figures, Melchizedek arrives fully formed—no birth narrative, no childhood exploits—then vanishes without a tombstone or obituary. This stark absence invites us to ask not just who he was but why Scripture withholds such basic biographical data. In exploring his "birth" through the lens of genealogical silence, his rule through the daily rhythms of Salem's worship and justice, and his "death" through narrative disappearance, we discover that the pattern of omission itself carries theological weight. What if the missing details signal that Melchizedek belongs to a higher order, one that transcends ordinary human lifespans? How might his priest-king life in a Canaanite city illuminate God's work in covenant hospitality, liturgical care, and peace-making? And what do ancient attempts—from rabbinic midrash to Second-Temple legends—to fill in his story tell us about communal yearnings for divine mediators? This chapter ventures into these questions, balancing historical reconstruction with literary sensitivity and theological insight, so that the life we piece together becomes a springboard into the mystery that Christ alone fully satisfies.

6.1.When Scripture Omits a Birth Certificate

6.1.1 Purpose of a Biographical Chapter in a Biography-less Narrative

 Although Melchizedek appears for mere moments in the Genesis account, the absence of any birth or death narrative transforms those fleeting verses into a theological canvas. By dedicating a chapter to his "life story" despite the lack of concrete data, we underscore how absence itself conveys meaning: divine prerogative over human history. Exploring his beginnings and endings—or lack thereof—reveals the ways Scripture uses silence to highlight eternal realities rather than temporal details. This chapter seeks to unpack the strategic significance of that narrative gap, showing how it redirects attention from lineage to office, from chronology to covenant. It also demonstrates that biblical biography need not replicate modern standards of comprehensive life-story but instead elevates key elements that serve redemptive purposes. By probing questions about Melchizedek's origins, upbringing, and departure, we invite readers into the tension between historical curiosity and theological reflection. Such a biographical study becomes a springboard for understanding God's method of self-revelation through selected snapshots rather than exhaustive catalogs. In doing so, we prepare to analyze the paradox of genealogical silence in Section 2. The lack of a birth certificate thus becomes a focal point, challenging us to embrace narrative omission as a divine signpost directing us toward the eternal priest-king's true identity.

6.1.2 Method: Historical Possibility, Literary Function, Theological Payoff

To investigate a figure whose personal details are intentionally withheld, we employ a three-pronged method. First, we explore historical possibilities, examining archaeological and cultural evidence for analogous figures in second-millennium B.C. Canaan to construct a plausible sketch of Melchizedek's milieu. This approach respects the ancient Near Eastern context without conflating hypothesis with canonical authority. Second, we analyze the literary function of omission: by omitting birth and death, the Genesis author communicates that Melchizedek's priesthood transcends mortal constraints. Literary studies show that narrative gaps often serve as theological signals, inviting midrashic expansion and reader participation. Third, we assess the theological payoff: silence in Scripture often magnifies divine mystery, prompting reflection on topics like eternal priesthood, covenant mediation, and the anticipation of the Messiah. This theological lens considers how New Testament writers, particularly in Hebrews 7:3, treat the same silences as typological indicators. By interweaving these dimensions—historical plausibility, literary strategy, and theological significance—we honor both the text's ancient setting and its canonical trajectory. This methodological foundation equips us to examine the paradox of genealogical silence in the next section, ensuring our study remains balanced between inquiry and reverent interpretation.

6.2. The Paradox of Genealogical Silence

6.2.1 Genealogy as Legitimacy in the Ancient Near East

In the ancient Near East, genealogies functioned as the backbone of social and religious legitimacy, establishing one's right to land, office, and priestly privileges. Royal inscriptions from Mari and Ugarit routinely trace kings' ancestry back to divine ancestors or founding patriarchs, signaling unbroken continuity of authority. Temple personnel lists from Ebla and Nuzi similarly catalog priestly families, emphasizing the hereditary nature of cultic service. Within Israel, explicit genealogies in Chronicles and Ezra–Nehemiah codify priestly lines from Aaron and Levi, preserving purity of cultic transmission (1 Chr 6:1–81; Neh 12:1–26). By contrast, Melchizedek lacks any recorded lineage, birthdate, or genealogy, creating a paradox: a priest without ancestral credentials in a culture that valued them above almost all else. This absence disrupts expectations, forcing readers to ponder why the narrator would intentionally bypass a key legitimizing detail. The silence suggests that Melchizedek's authority derives not from human descent but from divine appointment—an authority greater than ordinary pedigree. In ancient context, such a radical omission would have jarred contemporary audiences, sharpening awareness that this priest-king operates on a different plane. This paradox lays the groundwork for exploring narrative strategy and theological intent in the next subsections.

6.2.2 Deliberate Omission as Narrative Strategy in Genesis

Genesis 14's brief account of Melchizedek immediately follows Abram's rescue of Lot, yet the text pauses only to note Melchizedek's titles and actions, never his origins. This focused storytelling serves as a strategic literary move: by spotlighting Melchizedek's priestly blessing and Abraham's tithe, the narrator draws attention to covenantal dynamics rather than family pedigree. The omission functions like a narrative spotlight, illuminating theological themes of blessing, sovereignty, and priestly mediation. Literary scholars observe that such ellipses are not accidental but carefully calibrated to convey what matters most: divine election and redemptive encounter. Moreover, the abrupt exit that follows the encounter underscores that the significance lies in the event, not in the biography. This strategy sets Melchizedek apart from other Genesis characters whose lineage and lifespan are meticulously recorded, signaling that his priesthood transcends normal human categories. The narrative thus crafts a sense of otherness, preparing the ground for New Testament readers to interpret Melchizedek as a type of Christ. In this way, deliberate omission in Genesis shapes theological reading across centuries, as we will see in Hebrews and elsewhere.

6.2.3 How Silence Becomes a Theological Shout in Hebrews 7

Hebrews 7:3 transforms narrative silence into explicit theology: "He is without father or mother or genealogy, having neither beginning of days nor end of life." The author of Hebrews interprets Genesis's omission as typological proof of an eternal priesthood—one that aligns perfectly with Christ's own timeless mediation. What Genesis leaves unspoken, Hebrews proclaims with clarity, using the absence of genealogical data to signify immortality and perpetual ministry. This theological appropriation demonstrates how early Christians read Scripture through a Christ-centered lens, finding fulfillment in Christ's person and work. The silence in Genesis thus becomes a theological shout in Hebrews, announcing that Christ's priesthood, like Melchizedek's, requires no human credentials. The author's bold reinterpretation reveals the canonical interplay between texts: an Old Testament narrative lacuna feeds New Testament doctrinal insight. This transformative use of silence underscores the unity of Scripture's redemptive message and prepares readers to dwell on Melchizedek's deeper mysteries, as explored in subsequent chapters.

6.3. Ancient Attempts to Supply a Birth Story

6.3.1 Rabbinic Identification with Shem: Midrashic Motives

 Early rabbinic midrash often sought to fill the blank slate of Melchizedek's origins by identifying him with Shem, Noah's son. Targum Pseudo-Jonathan explicitly names Shem as the priest-king of Salem, merging genealogical memory with patriarchal prestige. This identification serves midrashic motives: by linking Melchizedek to Shem, the rabbis preserve monotheistic continuity from Noah's righteous line through Abraham, reinforcing the universality of God's covenant. Such midrash emphasizes that true priesthood transcends ethnic Israel, rooting it in the human family represented by Noah's lineage. The midrash also provides a convenient solution to the narrative puzzle of Melchizedek's absence of ancestry, restoring a sense of continuity for Jewish audiences who valued genealogical records. Moreover, by making Shem and Melchizedek the same person, the rabbinic tradition underscores the timeless nature of priestly mediation, anticipating later Christian appropriation. These rabbinic attempts illustrate how communal storytelling addressed textual silences, shaping interpretive traditions that resonate in the pagodas of scriptural engagement.

6.3.2 Second-Temple Legends of Pre-Nativity Vows

 Intertestamental texts outside Qumran, such as the Book of Jubilees and other pseudepigrapha, narrate legendary accounts of Melchizedek's youth, crafting stories of vows taken before his birth. According to one fragmentary tradition, his mother vowed him to lifelong service if she survived childbirth, and that vow imbued him with divine grace from the womb. These legends dramatize the notion that Melchizedek's priesthood is ordained from conception, reinforcing themes of predestination and election. They also align with broader Second-Temple interests in exemplary righteous figures whose lives foreshadow the end-time deliverer. While not canonical, these narratives reveal a communal appetite for personal details that Genesis intentionally withholds. They also connect with broader Mediterranean birth-vow tropes, where infants dedicate their lives to temple service, echoing Naziritic or consecration motifs. These legends underscore how ancient communities used creative storytelling to bridge gaps in Scripture, even as later interpreters would treat such tales with caution. The layering of these narratives onto the skeletal Genesis fragment demonstrates the rich tapestry of Jewish imagination in the centuries before Christ.

6.3.3 Patristic Proposals of Pre-Incarnate Manifestation

The early church Fathers, from Irenaeus to Athanasius, proposed that Melchizedek's appearance in Genesis was a Christophany—a visible manifestation of the pre-incarnate Son. Irenaeus argues that the Logos appeared to Abraham in priestly garb, blessing him as God Most High, thus prefiguring the incarnation (Against Heresies IV.20). Athanasius expands this by suggesting that Melchizedek's lack of genealogy indicates divine rather than human origin, a sign that the eternal Word temporarily clothed Himself in human form. Such patristic proposals reflect Christological priorities: by interpreting Melchizedek as Christ, the Fathers demonstrate continuity of the Son's mediatorial work from before creation to after resurrection. This interpretation repurposes the birth narrative question into a theological statement: Christ's priesthood has no beginning in time. While modern scholarship tends to view these as theological readings rather than historical claims, they reveal how the early church engaged Genesis's silences to affirm the doctrine of Christ's eternality and incarnation. These patristic voices thus offer a window into the formative centuries when Melchizedek's mystery became central to articulating Jesus's divine identity.

6.4. Melchizedek's Formative Years— Historical Reconstructions

6.4.1 Jebusite Royal Education: Scribal Training and Temple Rites

If Melchizedek was a historical Jebusite monarch, he would likely have undergone formal royal education typical of city-state rulers around 2000 B.C. Such education involved scribal training in cuneiform administration, including record-keeping for tribute, legal contracts, and cultic inventories. He may have studied hymns and liturgies to lead temple ceremonies, mastering ritual languages and techniques for offerings. His instruction would also include diplomatic protocol, enabling him to negotiate treaties and tithe arrangements—skills demonstrated in his interaction with Abraham. As a priest-king, he needed proficiency in the rituals of the Canaanite high god, possibly adapted to monotheistic worship of El Elyon. Archaeological parallels at Ugarit and Hazor reveal palace chapels where young royals learned sacrificial procedures. Such reconstruction situates Melchizedek within a plausible educational context, blending political and religious pedagogy. It also highlights the intimate link between scribal culture and priesthood in ancient urban centers, where literacy served both administration and cult. Understanding these formative elements prepares us to envision how Melchizedek exercised his dual office in Salem's sacred precincts, which we explore next.

6.4.2 Regional Politics of Salem: Trade Corridors and Diplomatic Skill

Salem's geographic position atop the ridge west of the Jordan placed it at a crossroads of trade between Egypt's Sinai routes and Mesopotamian arteries. Control of these corridors conferred economic power, requiring the ruler to deftly balance alliances with neighboring city-states and more powerful kingdoms. Melchizedek would have needed diplomatic acumen to negotiate safe passage for caravans, secure favorable tariffs, and extract tithes or tributes without provoking hostilities. His encounter with Abraham after the latter's victory over regional coalitions suggests an awareness of intertribal power dynamics and the ability to broker mutual recognition. Such political skill meant cultivating relationships with both nomadic groups and settled polities, ensuring Salem's security and prosperity. Furthermore, his dual role likely included overseeing regional dispute resolution, where judgments at the city gate (gateway justice) reinforced his authority. This political dimension underscores that his priestly blessing carried tangible weight in international affairs. By reconstructing Salem's political landscape, we appreciate the complexity of Melchizedek's leadership, which seamlessly integrated spiritual and civic responsibilities. This foundation invites us next to examine the specifics of his cultic praxis amid Canaanite syncretism.

6.4.3 Cultic Praxis under Canaanite Syncretism—A Monotheistic Hold-out?

Canaanite religion in the Middle Bronze Age featured a pantheon led by El and Baal, with local high places dedicated to various deities. Yet Melchizedek's designation as "priest of El Elyon" suggests a focus on the high god, possibly indicating monolatric rather than full polytheistic practice. His role may have involved reformist impulses, emphasizing the supremacy of El Elyon over lesser gods—a theological stance echoed in Abraham's own worship. Archaeological remains of high places often show altars and standing stones; Melchizedek's cultic duties would include maintaining these sacred sites, conducting animal offerings, and leading liturgical feasts. The possibility of syncretism—blending Canaanite motifs with emerging Israelite monotheism—raises questions about the purity of his worship. Yet the Genesis narrative frames his priesthood as wholly aligned with "God Most High," distinguishing him from local cults. This tension between shared cultural forms and theological distinctiveness illustrates how Melchizedek's ministry may have served as a bridge between pagan surroundings and covenantal fidelity.

His monotheistic hold-out offers a portrait of charismatic leadership rooted in divine revelation amid prevailing religious pluralism. With these facets of his formative and ministerial context in view, we stand prepared to explore how his singular actions—the celebrated bread-and-wine encounter—epitomize his priest-king legacy.

6.5. Life and Rule in Salem: Daily Rhythms of a Priest-King

6.5.1 Liturgical Calendar: Harvest Festivals, New-Moon Rites, and Covenant Meals

As king of Salem and priest of El Elyon, Melchizedek would have overseen a liturgical calendar centering on agricultural cycles—especially the spring barley and autumn wheat harvests. These festivals, akin to Israel's later Feasts of Unleavened Bread and Ingathering (Exodus 23:14–16), likely involved communal offerings of first fruits and thanksgiving sacrifices. New-moon rites, celebrating the turn of each lunar cycle, would have combined ceremonial incense, trumpet blasts, and communal meals at a high-place altar—practices attested in Numbers 10:10 and Psalm 81:3. As host of covenant meals, Melchizedek presided over sacrificial feasts that bound participants into social and divine covenants, mirroring Abraham's tithe and fellowship (Genesis 14:18–20). These gatherings reinforced collective identity under El Elyon's sovereignty, promoting social cohesion and religious devotion. The ritual year would have included rites of purification linked to agrarian life—akin to Israel's Days of Atonement (Leviticus 16)—to maintain holiness in the community. Music and liturgical recitation of hymns may have accompanied each festival, with the priest-king leading psalm-like compositions celebrating divine providence. Seasonal offerings of oil and wine—symbols of abundance—would underscore economic and spiritual reliance on the high god. Through these liturgical rhythms, Melchizedek's rule calibrated human time to divine eternity, foreshadowing the Christian liturgical year that marks Christ's paschal mystery.

This liturgical structure paved the way for justice functions, as festival gatherings also resolved disputes and integrated strangers into the community.

6.5.2 Judicial Functions: Gate-City Courts and Conflict Mediation

As ruler of a city-state, Melchizedek would have sat at the city gate to adjudicate disputes, a role reminiscent of Deborah's judgments under the palm of Deborah (Judges 4:5). His priestly office lent moral authority to his verdicts, ensuring that decisions reflected covenantal principles of justice (Deuteronomy 16:18–20). Litigants—whether local farmers contesting land boundaries or traders disputing caravan dues—would present their cases before him, expecting impartial resolution grounded in divine law. The integration of judicial and cultic functions meant that oaths sworn before El Elyon carried the weight of divine witness, deterring perjury and enforcing social order. In matters of ritual purity—such as handling sacrificial animals—he would ensure compliance with cultic regulations, paralleling the Levitical priest's oversight (Leviticus 10:10). Dispute mediation often involved ceremonial gestures, such as laying hands on the accused or on sacrificial animals, symbolizing transfer of guilt or blessing (Leviticus 1:4). His judgments likely included restitution measures—compensation in shekels or produce—reinforcing communal harmony. This judicial paradigm reflects Psalm 99:6's depiction of priest-judges who "called on your name, O Lord, and were saved." By combining sacrificial atonement with civic justice, Melchizedek's governance prefigured the Messiah's role as both judge and covenant mediator. His court thus functioned as a microcosm of cosmic order, where human conflict met divine arbitration.

6.5.3 Economy of Peace: Tithes, Tribute, and Redistribution

Under Melchizedek's rule, an "economy of peace" would regulate wealth through tithes, tribute, and redistribution, preventing both famine and inequality. As Abraham's simple tithe (Genesis 14:20) set a precedent, civic tribute likely took the form of a fixed percentage of harvest or trade goods, dedicated to the temple treasury. These resources funded the maintenance of worship spaces, care for the poor, and hospitality to travelers—echoing Deuteronomy 14:29's provision for Levites, strangers, orphans, and widows. Regular redistribution ceremonies—akin to Jubilee's debt release (Leviticus 25)—may have occurred to prevent entrenched poverty, promoting social stability and divine favor. Melchizedek's dual office meant that economic policies carried spiritual significance: giving became an act of worship, and consumption a reminder of reliance on El Elyon's provision. Craftsmen and artisans likely contributed part of their production to temple workshops, integrating economic productivity with cultic artistry. During lean years, stored tithes ensured famine relief, reflecting a divine guarantee of provision (Psalm 37:25). This deliberate redistribution fostered peace (shalom) by curbing exploitation and demonstrating covenantal solidarity. The priest-king's oversight of this system made his reign synonymous with both spiritual and material well-being. Such an integrated economy anticipates Christ's promise that God will supply "all our needs" (Philippians 4:19) and foreshadows the New Testament's emphasis on communal sharing (Acts 4:34–35). From these economic foundations, Melchizedek's hospitality to Abraham emerges as both diplomatic courtesy and ritual enactment of covenantal generosity.

6.6. The Bread-and-Wine Encounter Revisited (Genesis 14)

6.6.1 Military Diplomacy: Greeting a Victorious Patriarch

 Abram's return from battle against a confederation of kings placed him in a precarious political position, for victorious warlords often imposed tribute or enforced regional domination. Melchizedek's decision to greet Abram with bread and wine signified diplomatic recognition of Abram's victory as endorsed by El Elyon. This act functioned as an acknowledgment of political parity: neither retainer nor rival, Melchizedek extended hospitality to a foreign warlord while subtly asserting Salem's autonomy. In ancient Near Eastern diplomacy, sharing a meal sealed alliances, with bread symbolizing sharing of land and wine signifying unity of purpose. By offering these elements, Melchizedek initiated a covenant-like bond, prefiguring treaty rituals found in Hittite suzerainty texts. This gesture also avoided conflict escalation, transforming potential hostilities into mutual blessing. The military context thus infuses the bread-and-wine encounter with geopolitical resonance, highlighting Melchizedek's skillful balance of piety and statecraft. His diplomatic hospitality contrasts with reactive violence, modeling a peaceful resolution grounded in divine prerogative rather than brute force. This scene illustrates how priestly mediation and political negotiation converged in Melchizedek's office, setting a pattern for the ultimate peacemaking ministry of Christ.

6.6.2 Sacred Hospitality: Covenant Meal as Royal Treaty

The covenant meal offered by Melchizedek aligns with ancient treaty-meal customs, where host and guest drank wine mixed at the altar and shared bread as a sign of mutual commitment before their gods. In this context, the meal transcends mere sustenance—it embodies a binding agreement invoking divine witnesses. Bread, representing sustenance, signaled that neither party would resort to coercion, while wine, associated with joy and covenant memory, represented mutual delight in the agreement. In Melchizedek's offering, these elements acquired sacrificial meaning: the bread and wine were consecrated to El Elyon, sanctifying the encounter as both political pact and cultic rite. By using sacred hospitality to enact a royal treaty, Melchizedek wielded spiritual authority to secure peace and cooperation. This dual symbolism of hospitality and sacrifice resonates with Christian Eucharistic theology, where sharing bread and wine proclaims the new covenant (Luke 22:19–20). Thus, Melchizedek's covenant meal foreshadows Christ's sacrificial hospitality, inviting all nations into communion with the Most High. The sacred meal, as a royal treaty, underscores Melchizedek's unique capacity to unite political and spiritual realms under divine peace.

6.6.3 Blessing Formula Analysis: Syntax, Theology, Reciprocity

Melchizedek's blessing of Abram—"Blessed be Abram by God Most High, Possessor of heaven and earth; and blessed be God Most High, who has delivered your enemies into your hand"—follows a two-clause structure featuring reciprocating divine and human blessings (Genesis 14:19–20). The Hebrew syntax places divine blessing first, establishing El Elyon's priority, then connects Abram's right to receive blessing to God's sovereign action. The reciprocity—Melchizedek blessing Abram, and Abram in turn giving tithe—creates a covenant loop of divine-human exchange. The theological implication is that blessing flows from God to the faithful and then returns as human worship and obedience. This pattern contrasts with typical patron-client blessings, which often ended with human loyalty without explicit divine reciprocity. By emphasizing God's deliverance of Abram's enemies, the blessing acknowledges divine agency in military victory and redirects human triumph into worshipful gratitude. The formula's compact symmetry highlights covenant mutuality: divine grace elicits human response, which nets further divine favor. This blessing syntax prefigures New Testament thanksgiving hymns (e.g., Philippians 2:9–11) that celebrate Christ's exaltation, connecting Melchizedek's formula to the broader biblical tradition of reciprocal blessing. The strategic placement of this blessing in the narrative thus crystallizes its theological significance and sets the stage for Abraham's generous tithe.

6.7. Apparent Death—or the Art of Exiting the Stage

6.7.1 Literary Vanishing Acts in Biblical Narrative (e.g., Enoch, Elijah)

The abrupt disappearance of Melchizedek without death account parallels other biblical vanishings: Enoch "walked with God; then he was no more, because God took him" (Genesis 5:24) and Elijah ascended in a whirlwind (2 Kings 2:11). These literary vanishing acts signal divine election and extraordinary status, distinguishing the individuals from ordinary mortals. In each case, the figure's removal underscores their special relationship with God and hints at ongoing heavenly ministry. The narrative choice to eliminate any death record transforms mortality into mystery, inviting readers to view the missing death as signifier of ongoing life in divine presence. Such vanishing acts also foreshadow eschatological expectations of translation without experiencing decay. By placing Melchizedek's disappearance alongside Enoch and Elijah, the Genesis author aligns him with a tradition of those who bypass death's finality—a theme later amplified in Hebrews 7:3. These intertextual echoes equip interpreters to see Melchizedek's "vanishing" not as narrative oversight but as deliberate theological symbol. Recognizing this pattern across Scripture prepares us to explore the tension between deathless archetype and historical mortality.

6.7.2 Deathless Archetype versus Historical Mortality: Tension Explained

The motif of immortality in Melchizedek's description— "without end of life"—contrasts sharply with historical plausibility, since all human leaders eventually die. This tension highlights the text's typological intent: Melchizedek embodies an archetype of eternal priesthood, pointing beyond the bounds of ordinary human lifespan. The historical reality of mortality is thus transcended to foreshadow the Messiah's unending intercession. Readers encounter a figure who, though human, participates in divine life, challenging assumptions about death's inevitability. This tension also functions rhetorically, compelling readers to seek fulfillment in one "after the order of Melchizedek" whose life truly has no end (Hebrews 7:16). The unresolved paradox invites theological reflection: human life, when aligned with God's purposes, partakes of divine eternity. The archetypal narrative thus becomes a template for understanding Christ's resurrection and ascension, where mortality gives way to imperishable life (1 Corinthians 15:54–55). By embracing this tension, communities learn to hold human history and divine eschatology in creative dialectic, anticipating the day when death is swallowed up in victory (Revelation 21:4).

6.7.3 Jewish and Christian Speculations on Translation to Heaven

Jewish traditions—mystical and legend alike—speculate that Melchizedek, Enoch, and Elijah were "translated" to heavenly realms, continuing priestly service before God's throne. The Testament of Abraham (2nd century A.D.) recounts Abraham's heavenly vision of Melchizedek alive in the divine council, presiding over sacrifices and intercession. Early Christian writers like Justin Martyr and Origen similarly upheld that Melchizedek remains active in heaven, offering bread and wine before God. These speculations reflect a theology of translation—bodily assumption into divine presence— affirmed in the New Testament's presentation of Christ's ascension (Acts 1:9). The notion of ongoing heavenly ministry resonates with Hebrews 7:25's affirmation that Christ "always lives to make intercession." Such speculations provided believers with vivid imagery of a high priest whose work extends beyond temporal boundaries. While not empirically verifiable, these traditions shaped devotional imagination, reinforcing confidence in eternal mediation. They also bridged Old Testament narratives with Christian soteriology, aligning Melchizedek's "translation" with Christ's exaltation. As communities pondered these speculations, the boundaries between historical figure and heavenly archetype blurred, enriching worship and hope.

6.8. "Without End of Life": Immortality Motifs across Traditions

6.8.1 Qumran's Eternal Deliverer Versus Hebrews' Timeless High Priest

The Dead Sea Scroll 11QMelchizedek portrays him as an eschatological judge who, in the year of vengeance, delivers the righteous and binds the wicked—activities implying ongoing heavenly action. Qumran's Melchizedek is a cosmic agent whose life extends into the final age, reflecting a community's longing for an immortal deliverer. Hebrews, while not apocalyptic in the same sense, affirms Melchizedek's timeless priesthood as a type of Christ's perpetual intercession (Hebrews 7:3). The epistle reframes the Qumran deliverer motif into a christological paradigm: Jesus, like Melchizedek, shares no recorded beginning or end, guaranteeing unceasing mediation. Unlike Qumran's dual-messiah schema, Hebrews consolidates the roles of priest and judge in Christ alone. This canonical appropriation transforms sectarian expectations into a universal theological claim, offering believers a mediator whose life spans all ages. The intersection of these traditions illustrates how Second-Temple Jewish motifs inform early Christian soteriology while the church refines them into Christ-centered doctrine. Recognizing both streams enriches understanding of immortality motifs as they flow into New Covenant hope.

6.8.2 Kabbalistic Concepts of Olam Ha-Ba and the Living Tzaddiq

Medieval Kabbalah elaborates on immortality through concepts like *Olam Ha-Ba* (the World to Come) and the *Living Tzaddiq*—the righteous one who bridges heaven and earth. Melchizedek's timeless priesthood aligns with the *Living*

Tzaddiq, a soul whose merit sustains the cosmos through continuous prayer and divine service. Kabbalistic texts like the Zohar portray him as a celestial archetype maintaining the flow of divine light, prefiguring soul translocation in *Olam Ha-Ba*. His unending life becomes symbolic of the perfected spiritual state that awaits the faithful—an existence beyond physical decay. This mystical portrayal complements biblical hints of translation and eternal service, deepening Jewish eschatological vision. The Kabbalistic reading thus reimagines Melchizedek's silence on death as an invitation into ongoing cosmic liturgy, where ritual time yields to eternal present. This tradition enriches the dialogue between biblical narrative and mystical theology, demonstrating how Melchizedek's immortality resonates across streams of spiritual interpretation.

6.8.3 Medieval Christian Notions of the Wandering Priest-King

In medieval Christian lore, Melchizedek appears occasionally as a wandering priest-king, carrying his perpetual priesthood across distant lands without aging or death. Chronicles like the *Golden Legend* recount pilgrims meeting a venerable stranger who blesses them with bread and wine, vanishing before dawn—an allusion to Melchizedek's silent exit. These stories, while apocryphal, reflect the church's fascination with eternal sanctity and the hope for living intermediaries between heaven and earth. Monastic orders sometimes adopted Melchizedek as a patron, emphasizing vows of perpetual prayer and service. Such lore reinforced the notion of unbroken priestly lineage, even as institutional structures changed. By narrating a living priest-king traversing centuries, medieval Christians found a model of sanctity that transcended both life and death, mirroring Christ's eternal intercession. These narratives, while extra-canonical, shaped devotional imagination, inspiring believers to seek continuous fellowship with the living Lord. As we conclude this chapter, these varied immortality motifs demonstrate how Melchizedek's birthless and deathless portrait prompts enduring reflection on human mortality, divine eternity, and the hope of participation in an everlasting priesthood.

6.9. Theological Stakes of an Unrecorded Death

6.9.1 Eschatology: Prototype of Resurrection and Incorruptibility

Melchizedek's lack of recorded death functions as an eschatological prototype, pointing readers beyond mortal decay to resurrection hope. His narrative disappearance prefigures the promised reversal of death's finality, as celebrated in 1 Corinthians 15:54–55, where death is "swallowed up in victory." By withholding any mention of his demise, Scripture implies that Melchizedek participates in a mode of existence unbound by the grave—an existence that Christ fulfills through his resurrection and eternal life (Romans 6:9). This motif encourages believers to view death not as an ultimate endpoint but as a transformative passage into divine presence. The absence of burial also echoes Ezekiel 37's vision of dry bones revived, underscoring that God's creative power can raise life from apparent nothingness. In Revelation 21:4, where "death shall be no more," the pattern established by Melchizedek's unrecorded death finds its consummation in the new creation. As a narrative forerunner, Melchizedek embodies the community's eschatological expectation: that God's faithful will be clothed in incorruption and dwell eternally in unhindered communion (2 Timothy 1:10). His deathless portrait thus fuels Christian perseverance, assuring believers that their hope rests not on human longevity but on God's defeat of death. By connecting Genesis's silence with New Testament resurrection themes, the priest-king's story transcends its ancient context to speak powerfully into Christian eschatology.

6.9.2 Soteriology: Assurance Grounded in Undying Mediation

Melchizedek's apparent immortality also carries soteriological weight, as it models the undying mediation essential to human salvation. Just as Aaronic priests ceased with death and required successors, Melchizedek's priesthood, unbroken by mortality, anticipates the eternal intercession of Christ (Hebrews 7:25). His disappearance without burial implies that his priestly service continues perpetually before God's throne, offering an archetype for Christ's once-for-all sacrifice and ongoing advocacy. This serves as the basis for believers' assurance: salvation rests not on fluctuating human effort but on an imperishable High Priest whose ministry endures beyond death. The motif reinforces Romans 8:34's assertion that Christ "is at the right hand of God and is also interceding for us," establishing a soteriological anchor that no foe can dismantle. Furthermore, the absence of a human grave avoids any suggestion that mediation might lapse, contrasting with mortal mediators who cannot permanently secure forgiveness. This narrative strategy underscores that divine grace, once applied, remains valid for all generations. It also invites worshipers to approach God with confidence, knowing their salvation is guarded by a mediator whose life transcends time. In this light, Melchizedek's unrecorded death becomes the pre-figure of soteriological security that permeates the New Covenant.

6.9.3 Ecclesiology: Church as Community of the "Never-Dying" in Christ

The ecclesiological implications of Melchizedek's absent death resonate in the church's self-understanding as a community anchored in the "never-dying" life of Christ. In 1 Peter 2:9, believers are called "a chosen race, a royal priesthood," sharing in Christ's eternal priesthood—a status unassailable by death or adversity. Melchizedek's narrative silence on death thus models the church's identity: a spiritual body whose life derives from the living Head (Colossians 2:19). By emulating his perpetual ministry, the church affirms

147

that its worship, mission, and fellowship partake in divine continuity that outlasts temporal fracture. This ecclesiological vision informs sacraments, where baptism unites the faithful to Christ's death and resurrection (Romans 6:4), inaugurating participation in his undying life. It also shapes communal care, as members intercede for each other in the confidence that Christ's eternal ministry sustains their witness. The absence of a Melchizedek grave in Scripture thus invites the church to resist institutional models susceptible to decline, instead embracing a living embodiment of priestly-kingly service. In this sense, ecclesiology becomes eschatologically oriented, as the church lives now as a foretaste of the assembly that will gather eternally around Christ's unending priesthood. Melchizedek's unrecorded death thus undergirds a robust theology of the church's perpetual vocation.

6.10. Liturgical Echoes of Birth, Life, and Deathlessness

6.10.1 Baptismal Naming Rites and Melchizedek's Silent Genealogy

Early Christian baptismal rites often included a renaming element, symbolizing believers' new identity in Christ, unbound by ancestral lineage. This echoes Melchizedek's silent genealogy: just as his origins are unnoted, Christians are "born not of blood nor of the will of the flesh" but of the Spirit (John 1:13). In the Apostolic Tradition of Hippolytus, baptismal candidates are instructed to "put off" their former name and "take a new name," signifying entry into Christ's eternal priesthood. This liturgical act parallels Melchizedek's birthless depiction, underscoring that Christian identity rests on divine birth rather than human descent. Eastern rites connect this renaming with sprinkling of oil and invocation of the Holy Spirit, signifying participation in an unending priestly ministry (1 Peter 2:5). By aligning baptismal naming with Melchizedek's silent origins, liturgical tradition reaffirms that believers share in an ageless lineage marked by spiritual rebirth. The omission of genealogical detail in the baptismal text thus becomes a feature, not a flaw—highlighting the church's lineage traced to Christ alone. This liturgical motif sets the stage for Eucharistic reflections on the Living Bread, explored next.

6.10.2 Eucharistic Prefaces Celebrating the "Living Bread and Wine"

Eucharistic prayers—especially in Eastern Orthodox and Ambrosian rites—invoke Melchizedek when recounting salvation history, describing Christ's body and blood as "Living Bread" and "Living Wine." The Anaphora of St. Basil includes a preface referencing Melchizedek: "As that righteous priest Melchizedek brought bread and wine to Abraham, so also after the same manner did Your only-begotten Son offer Himself..." This liturgical echo transforms the ancient Canaanite meal into a perpetual thanksgiving for Christ's self-offering (Luke 22:19–20). The phrase "living bread" (John 6:51) captures the paradox of body and blood that impart eternal life. By emphasizing "living," the prayers link Christ's unending priesthood with his unvanquished life beyond death. The consecration thus becomes a participation in Melchizedek's archetypal act, renewed every liturgy. Western Mass collects similarly frame the Eucharist as "the life-giving body and precious blood" that "endure forever." These liturgical traditions underscore Melchizedek's deathlessness as realized in Christ's living presence among the faithful. The Eucharistic recitation of his name enshrines his mystery in communal worship, forging continuity between Genesis's silent prototype and the church's sacramental life. Having celebrated the living meal, attention turns to funeral rites that confront death's finality, yet invoke Melchizedek's deathless hope.

6.10.3 Funeral Liturgies Invoking a Priest-King Who Knows No Grave

Christian funeral rites often incorporate references to eternal life and resurrection, invoking Melchizedek's template to console the bereaved. In the Byzantine Orthros of the

149

Departed, petitions ask that the deceased "may be numbered among the citizens of the heavenly Salem" and "served by the eternal Priest." These prayers reconstruct Salem as an eschatological city where death has no dominion (Revelation 21:4). Western funeral Requiem Masses sing "Lux aeterna" (everlasting light), echoing the promise of a life beyond tomb—an indirect nod to the deathless archetype. Liturgical homilies frequently cite Hebrews 7:16–17, reminding mourners that Christ's priesthood, unlike human intermediaries, cannot end in death. Such references transform the funeral assembly into a proclamation of Melchizedekian hope: that death's sting is vanquished and believers partake in eternal priestly life. The rite's use of incense, candles, and eucharistic bread symbolizes passage from death to inexhaustible communion, aligning with Melchizedek's unbroken service. By invoking his priest-king figure, funeral liturgies frame Christian mortality within an overarching narrative of immortality, offering both doctrinal clarity and pastoral comfort. The rhythmic recurrence of these themes in liturgy reinforces communal memory of the deathless mediator.

6.11. Ethical Implications: Living as People of an Unfinished Story

6.11.1 Identity beyond Ancestry—Hospitality and Justice Today

In a world fixated on lineage, Melchizedek's silent pedigree liberates believers from ancestry-based identity, redirecting focus to actions of hospitality and justice. Modern communities can draw inspiration from his model by prioritizing care for strangers, as Abraham's tithe and meal demonstrate (Genesis 14:20). Hospitality ministries— welcoming refugees, feeding the hungry, sheltering the homeless—embody this ethic, showing divine love without regard for background. Legal advocacy for the oppressed and impartial dispute mediation reflect his judicial functions (Genesis 14:18). By imitating Melchizedek's integrated role,

Christians resist narrow tribalism and cultivate inclusive communities. Churches can adopt policies ensuring fair distribution of resources, echoing his covenant economy of peace. This identity beyond ancestry fosters social cohesion and counters divisive ideologies. It also prompts reflection on how spiritual genealogy transcends ethnic and cultural barriers, uniting diverse peoples under one priest-king. In doing so, communities live out the legacy of an unfinished story, writing new chapters of compassion and justice. This ethical horizon leads naturally into leadership lessons drawn from a life hidden yet potent.

6.11.2 Leadership Lessons from a Life Hidden in God

Melchizedek's anonymity models servant leadership rooted in divine calling rather than personal fame. Contemporary leaders can learn to prioritize mission over recognition, performing crucial tasks without seeking credit. His hidden life—known only through a brief narrative—reminds executives and pastors that effectiveness does not require constant visibility. Strategic actions taken quietly can yield transformative outcomes, much like his blessing shifted Abraham's trajectory. This teaches that integrity and humility are hallmarks of authentic authority. Leaders should anchor decisions in principles rather than ambition, ensuring policies serve communal welfare. Ethical governance, like Melchizedek's, integrates spiritual values into public life, balancing compassion with justice. By embracing a hidden posture, leaders resist ego-driven agendas and cultivate trust. Mentorship models also emerge: guiding successors behind the scenes rather than dominating limelight. This hidden leadership echoes Christ's own humility (Philippians 2:5–7), reinforcing that true greatness lies in sacrificial service. These lessons shape organizational cultures that value substance over style, preparing communities for hope-filled mortality.

6.11.3 Hope-Filled Mortality: Facing Death under the Sign of Melchizedek

Melchizedek's absent demise invites Christians to embrace mortality with hope rather than fear, viewing life as a pilgrimage toward divine presence. Funerals rooted in his archetype transform death from a curse into a threshold of eternal communion. Pastoral care can draw from his deathless symbolism to comfort the grieving, emphasizing that earthly separation is temporary. End-of-life ministry then becomes not only a support for dying individuals but a celebration of life's continuation in God's care. This perspective encourages proactive engagement with mortality—wills, legacy projects, ethical memorials—ensuring that one's life story, though unfinished on earth, contributes to communal flourishing. It also fosters intergenerational solidarity, as older members transmit wisdom under the sign of enduring priesthood. Facing death with hope reshapes healthcare ethics, promoting palliative care that balances dignity and spiritual accompaniment. Ultimately, Melchizedek's example reframes mortality as invitation rather than tragedy, inviting believers to entrust their final chapter to the everlasting High Priest. This ethic anchors hope in God's unbroken covenant promises, sustaining faith through life's final passage.

Conclusion

Our journey through the empty cradle, the bustling citadel, and the silent grave of Melchizedek reveals that the power of his story lies less in chronological detail than in the contours of absence that Scripture intentionally preserves. His missing pedigree amplifies the message of an eternal priesthood unbound by human lineage; his modeled hospitality and justice foreshadow the universal reign of the true King-Priest; and his narrative disappearance gestures toward a life—and a hope—that transcends mortal constraints. Having traced how communities across eras have both filled in and revered these gaps, we see that biography becomes a vector for eschatological promise. As we turn to the next chapter, we will explore how participation in Melchizedek's legacy through sacrament, ethics, and mission invites every believer into the unfolding drama of a priestly people called to live between memory and consummation.

Chapter 7: Melchizedek and Christ

The life of Christ can only be fully understood against the backdrop of the mysterious priest-king of Salem. Melchizedek's brief yet potent appearance in the pages of Genesis and the Psalms serves as a theological foil against which Jesus reveals His unique identity. As we trace the contours of Melchizedek's shadow—his crown, his altar, his timeless service—we discover that every facet of Jesus's ministry, from His sacrificial offering to His authoritative teaching, finds its deepest meaning in the convergence of these two figures. This chapter weaves together biblical types, liturgical practice, and ethical vision to show how Christ does not merely repeat Melchizedek's role but transcends it, ushering in a kingdom where priestly intercession and sovereign rule coalesce in a single Person.

7.1. The Convergence of Two Names

7.1.1 Why Christology Requires Melchizedek and Vice-Versa

The figure of Melchizedek emerges in Scripture as both a king and priest, roles that in Christ converge perfectly in one Person. Without Melchizedek's archetype, the fullness of Jesus's priest-king ministry remains only half-seen. Conversely, without Christ's fulfillment, Melchizedek remains a tantalizing but incomplete type. Hebrews underscores this by citing Psalm 110:4—"You are a priest forever after the order of Melchizedek"—and applying it decisively to Jesus (Heb 5:6). This connection roots Christ's authority in an ancient pattern that predates the Aaronic line, legitimizing His unique mediation. Moreover, Christology gains traction when anchored in living biblical types rather than abstract categories. Melchizedek embodies covenant hospitality, sacrificial blessing, and eternal intercession—elements that Christ amplifies. By examining their relationship, theology honors both God's ancient promises and their ultimate realization. This dual focus also safeguards against reducing Jesus to a mere fulfillment of Mosaic foreshadowing; it highlights a priesthood that transcends Law and Temple. For the church's witness, the integration of Melchizedek and Christ furnishes a rich vocabulary for preaching, worship, and ethics. It also equips believers to articulate a holistic vision of salvation that embraces both atonement and reign. Recognizing this mutual necessity anchors our ensuing exploration in both Testaments, preparing us to map the typological matrix where their stories intersect.

7.1.2 From Ancient Salem to Global Church—Scope of the Chapter

Our journey begins in the hilltop city of Salem, whose fleeting appearance in Genesis 14 initiates a narrative trajectory reaching the ends of the earth. From that remote setting we traverse the psalmist's throne room (Psalm 110), the prophetic visions of Zechariah, the pages of Hebrews, and the liturgies of every continent. This chapter thus spans a vast theological geography, showing how an obscure priest-king becomes the universal Savior-Ruler. We will trace typology through Scripture, unpack key Christological titles from multiple biblical witnesses, and examine the practical outworking of Christ's dual office in worship and ethics. High-priestly themes of sacrifice and intercession will illuminate the depth of Jesus's atoning work, while royal motifs will shape our understanding of Kingdom ethics and mission. The chapter further engages sacramental continuity, demonstrating the living participation of believers in Christ's eternal priesthood. Through case studies in mission and spiritual warfare, we see how Christ's Melchizedekian identity sustains the church amid cultural fragmentation. Finally, we contemplate eschatological consummation, where New Jerusalem embodies the fullness of priest-king reign. By surveying this breadth, readers will appreciate how a brief Genesis encounter informs the global church's faith, praxis, and hope. The scope of our study thus mirrors the scope of Melchizedek's legacy—ancient in origin, eternal in reach.

7.2. Typological Matrix: Old-Testament Lines that Meet in Jesus

7.2.1 Genesis 14, Psalm 110, and Zechariah 6 on a Single Canvas

Genesis 14 introduces Melchizedek as "king of Salem" and "priest of God Most High" who blesses Abram with bread and wine (Gen 14:18–20). Psalm 110 builds on this, declaring the Lord's Anointed a permanent priest "after the order of Melchizedek" (Ps 110:4). Zechariah 6's vision of crowns on the head of the high priest Joshua resonates faintly with this royal-priestly motif (Zech 6:12–13), suggesting an enduring hope for a unified office. When these texts are laid side by side, a clear typological pattern emerges: a divinely appointed figure combining sovereign rule, sacrificial service, and covenant mediation. Genesis 14 provides the raw material,

Psalm 110 rings the typological bell, and Zechariah adds the expectation of liturgical restoration. The New Testament then weaves these strands into the person of Christ, who embodies the title "king of righteousness" (Heb 7:2) and "prince of peace" (Isa 9:6). This typological matrix demonstrates Scripture's unity, as early glimpses find their full meaning in Jesus. It also legitimates the church's proclamation by rooting Christology in the inspired witness of multiple canonical books. When believers encounter Christ as King-Priest, they stand at the intersection of these ancient lines. Appreciating the convergence of Genesis, Psalms, and Zechariah enhances both devotional reading and scholarly reflection. This matrix thus serves as the foundation for exploring the logic of fulfillment in the next subsection.

7.2.2 Shadow, Sketch, and Substance—Logic of Fulfillment

Biblical typology often progresses from shadow to sketch to substance: the ritual shadows of Levitical sacrifice outline the reality sketched by Melchizedek, which Christ then embodies fully. Shadows—like burnt offerings—point ahead but lack transformative power (Heb 10:1). Melchizedek's brief sketch in Genesis adds theological nuance: bread and wine signify covenant meal and priestly service. Psalm 110 amplifies the sketch with royal-priestly language, preparing readers for a figure greater than Aaron. Christ's ministry then actualizes these patterns: His body broken, blood poured, and ascension to heaven render the sketch into substance. This logic of fulfillment affirms that typology is not a puzzle to be deconstructed but a narrative arc to be embraced. Every shadow and sketch finds its true home in the historical person of Jesus, who both transcends and validates the ancient types. The fulfillment principle underscores God's faithfulness in orchestrating history to reveal Messiah. It also guards against supersessionism that discards Old Testament forms; instead, it integrates them into a living tapestry. For the church, understanding this logic enriches preaching and worship, as each ritual and text participates in Christ's reality.

With the fulfillment paradigm in view, we now turn to how Christological titles fit into this typological matrix.

7.2.3 Continuity without Redundancy: How Christ Surpasses the Types

While Christ's identity as priest and king requires continuity with Melchizedek's type, He also inaugurates a superior order that renders previous forms redundant in their provisional roles. The continuity affirms God's consistent purpose: the Melchizedek pattern fulfills in Christ what it foreshadowed. At the same time, the New Testament asserts that the old shadows have served their purpose and now must yield to substance (Heb 8:13). Christ's priesthood, founded on an oath (Ps 110:4), contrasts with the fragile, hereditary Aaronic tenure. His sacrifice, once for all, replaces daily blood offerings (Heb 10:10–14). His kingship, inaugurated at the resurrection and ascension, unites cosmic authority with pastoral care (Eph 1:20–23). This surpassing does not negate the types but fulfills them in a way no human successor could. The church honors this by preserving liturgical echoes— Eucharist, reading of Genesis 14 and Psalm 110—while affirming their true object in Christ. This seamless continuity without redundancy exemplifies divine economy: each stage builds toward fullness. Recognizing both the link and the leap prepares believers to embrace Christ's unique office, which we explore through specific titles in the next section.

7.3. Christological Titles in Melchizedekian Perspective

7.3.1 "King of Righteousness" and the Just One (Acts 3:14)

Melchizedek's title "king of righteousness" (Heb 7:2) resonates deeply with Peter's proclamation of Jesus as "the righteous one" whom Israel had disowned (Acts 3:14). In Jewish expectation, righteousness signified covenant fidelity and divine vindication. When Peter calls Christ "the righteous one," he identifies Jesus as the ultimate fulfilment of every righteous king, including Melchizedek and David. Jesus's life, free from sin (1 John 3:5), embodies perfect conformity to God's law—something the Levitical priests could not claim. As "king of righteousness," Christ not only rules but also restores justice, vindicating the poor and oppressed (Isa 42:1). His ministry inaugurates a reign where divine justice flows like a mighty stream (Amos 5:24). The courtroom scene of Melchizedek blessing Abram finds its climax in Christ's declaration: "The Son of Man has authority on earth to forgive sins" (Mark 2:10). This fusion of priestly mediation and royal justice underlines Christ's uniqueness. By embracing the title "righteous king," the church affirms both Christ's sinlessness and His enactment of God's covenant justice. It also shapes Christian ethics, calling believers to pursue righteousness as citizens of His kingdom. As we next consider "king of peace," we see these titles linking character and calling in Christ's reign.

7.3.2 "King of Peace" and the Prince of Peace (Isaiah 9:6)

Isaiah's proclamation of a child given the name "Prince of Peace" (Isa 9:6) dovetails with Melchizedek's designation as "king of peace" (Heb 7:2). Peace in Hebrew (*shalom*) denotes wholeness, prosperity, and reconciliation—dimensions fully realized in Christ's ministry. Jesus's birth—heralded by angels—ushers in peace on earth and goodwill toward humanity (Luke 2:14). His Sermon on the Mount blesses peacemakers, revealing that the kingdom of God advances through nonviolent reconciliation (Matt 5:9). At the cross, Christ defeats hostility by reconciling sinners to God (Col 1:20), fulfilling Melchizedek's archetype of covenant mediator. In His resurrection, Christ conquers the powers of death and chaos, inaugurating cosmic peace (1 Cor 15:55–57). The title "Prince of Peace" thus complements "king of righteousness," showing that Christian reign unites justice with mercy. As believers proclaim peace, they enact the royal priesthood's mission to bring shalom to broken communities. Liturgical prayers—such as the Agnus Dei—invoke Christ's peace, echoing Isaiah and Melchizedek's combined roles. Through this title, the church receives both comfort in suffering and commission for peacemaking. These royal-peace motifs set the stage for the Son of God and Son of Man synthesis explored next.

7.3.3 Son of God, Son of Man, and the Priest-King Synthesis

Christ's dual titles "Son of God" and "Son of Man" converge Melchizedekian elements: divine sonship affirms priestly election, while human sonship grounds royal solidarity. Psalm 2:7's "You are my Son" becomes a Christological oath at the resurrection (Heb 1:5). Daniel 7:13–14's "one like a son of man" receives dominion over all peoples, uniting kingship with cosmic judgment. Jesus repeatedly applies the Son of Man title to Himself, signaling both humility—identifying with humanity—and exaltation—receiving universal authority (Mark 14:62). In the parable of the sheep and goats, the Son of Man judges and intercedes, seamlessly blending priest-king functions (Matt 25:31–46). This synthesis roots Christ's mission in both divine initiative and human solidarity, fulfilling Melchizedek's pattern. By styling Himself Son of God and Son of Man, Jesus claims the fullness of Melchizedek's title cluster—righteousness, peace, and covenant mediation. The church proclaims this synthesis in creedal affirmations and baptismal formulas, embedding it at the heart of Christian identity. Recognizing this integrated Christology equips disciples to live under a sovereign Priest-King who fully represents both God and humanity. With these titles established, we now investigate Christ's high-priestly ministry and atoning work.

7.4. High-Priestly Ministry and Atonement

7.4.1 Once-for-All Sacrifice versus Daily Offerings (Hebrews 10:11–14)

Under the old covenant, priests offered sacrifices daily, year after year, yet each animal's death fell short of perfecting the worshipers (Heb 10:1–4). Christ's single offering, by contrast, suffices for all time—once for all—because He is both sinless and divine (Heb 7:27). Hebrews 10:11–14 contrasts the impotent repetition of Levitical sacrifice with the efficacy of Jesus's atonement: "For by a single offering He has perfected for all time those who are being sanctified." This once-for-all dimension underscores Christ's superiority over every previous system, including Melchizedek's prototype. His death secures definitive forgiveness, removing the need for continual ritual, yet establishes perpetual access to God. Liturgical memory in the Eucharist proclaims this sacrifice, not as a new repetition, but as the singular event with eternal efficacy. The pattern of daily offerings thus gives way to the one true offering, freeing the church from cultic repetition and directing faith to rest in Christ alone. This shift reorients worship: believers participate not in a cyclical system but in the definitive work of the Priest-King. The once-for-all concept also informs pastoral care, assuring the doubting that no sin remains unaddressed by Jesus's sacrifice. Having demonstrated the incomparable nature of Christ's atonement, we now consider His ongoing ministry of intercession.

7.4.2 Intercession, Advocacy, and the Throne of Grace (Hebrews 4:14–16)

Having offered Himself once, Christ ascends and continually ministers at the Father's right hand, making intercession for believers (Heb 7:25). Hebrews 4:14–16 invites Christians to approach the throne of grace with confidence, "that we may receive mercy and find grace in time of need." This advocacy parallels Melchizedek's priestly intercession, yet on a cosmic scale. No sin or struggle lies outside Christ's empathy, for He sympathizes with human weakness (Heb 4:15). His ongoing ministry sustains believers in temptation and trial, securing their perseverance. The throne of grace thus becomes a dynamic locus of worship and petition, contrasting with a static temple sanctuary. Christ's advocacy also integrates judicial and merciful roles: He pleads on behalf of His people while judging sin's root. This dual function reflects the priest-king model, where mercy and justice coalesce in one office. The assurance of access undergirds Christian prayer life, fostering boldness in seeking God's help. Pastoral theology draws from this intercession motif to encourage communal prayer, confident that the High Priest upholds every petition. Having examined His intercessory role, we proceed to the comprehensive scope of redemption Christ secures.

7.4.3 Cleansing Both Conscience and Cosmos— Scope of Redemption

Christ's priesthood cleanses believers' consciences from dead works, enabling service to the living God (Heb 9:14). This inner purification parallels the cosmic cleansing inaugurated by His reign, which reconciles all things to God (Col 1:20). The dual scope—personal sanctification and universal restoration—embodies Melchizedek's combined office. By entering the heavenly sanctuary with His own blood, Jesus inaugurates a new creation, inviting humanity into God's presence (Heb 9:12–13). His work removes barriers not only in human hearts but in the very structure of reality, defeating the powers of darkness (Col 2:15). This cosmic priesthood positions believers as agents of reconciliation in a broken world (2 Cor 5:18–20). Ethical transformation follows, as those cleansed in conscience now reflect divine character in society. The cosmic dimension of redemption fuels missional engagement, empowering the church to extend Christ's priestly ministry outward. Liturgical celebration and sacramental life thus anticipate the full restoration to come— when all creation sings under Christ's eternal reign. Having surveyed the atoning and restorative scope, the chapter turns next to the practical ethics of reigning under the Melchizedekian King.

7.5. Kingship Now: Ethics of a Melchizedekian Reign

7.5.1 Beatitudes as Royal Edict for Kingdom Citizens

The Beatitudes (Matthew 5:3–12) function as a royal decree issued by the Priest-King, calling His citizens to embody the values of the new reign. When Jesus pronounces "Blessed are the poor in spirit," He enacts the justice implicit in Melchizedek's title "king of righteousness," elevating humility over worldly power. "Blessed are those who mourn" reveals the merciful heart of the king, promising comfort to those who grieve injustice and loss. The peacemakers receive blessing by right of their participation in the "king of peace" ministry (Isa 9:6), carrying his mission of reconciliation into fractured communities. "Blessed are the meek" subverts assertions of force, echoing Melchizedek's example of peaceful authority. By promising inheritance of the earth, Jesus redefines royal succession—citizens share in divine dominion through righteousness and mercy. The Beatitudes' four-fold "blessed are" pattern crafts an ethical charter that stands in contrast to imperial edicts based on coercion. Each blessing aligns with a Melchizedekian virtue: poverty of spirit, mourning, meekness, hunger for justice, mercy, purity of heart, peacemaking, and perseverance under persecution. These are not optional ideals but prerequisites for participation in Christ's reign. The ethical reversal inherent in the Beatitudes proclaims a subversive kingdom where the last become first. In living these attitudes, believers enact their royal citizenship, demonstrating the practical implications of a Melchizedekian kingship on earth. As communities internalize these decrees, they transition naturally to public theology, the subject of the next section.

7.5.2 Justice, Mercy, and Peacemaking in Public Theology

The public witness of Christ's priest-kingdom demands structures and policies rooted in justice, mercy, and peacemaking. Justice, as envisioned by Melchizedek's reign, aligns with biblical mandates to "execute judgment in the morning" (Zeph 3:5), ensuring that societal goods flow equitably. Mercy tempers justice, reflecting the compassionate intercession of the eternal High Priest (Heb 7:25) and extending forgiveness to the marginalized. Peacemaking emerges as active reconciliation—bridging ethnic divisions, economic disparities, and political conflicts—mirroring Jesus's ministry that healed bodies and restored relationships (Matt 9:35–36). Public theology shaped by this triad rejects systems that exploit the poor, invade personal dignity, or foment violence. It calls legislators to craft laws that protect refugees, ensure fair wages, and uphold human rights in deference to God's image-bearers (James 2:1–9). Corporate policies and NGO programs become liturgical acts when informed by Melchizedekian ethics, offering hospitality and restitution rather than retribution. Justice ministries can draw on Levitical principles of gleaning (Lev 19:9–10) to address modern food insecurity, while mercy ministries apply Jesus's parable of the Good Samaritan (Luke 10:30–37) to refugee resettlement. Peacemaking initiatives, such as restorative justice circles, embody the Beatitude promise of shalom in tangible ways. This holistic public theology challenges the church to be salt and light (Matt 5:13–16), transforming social structures from the inside out. By advancing justice, mercy, and peace, believers demonstrate the practical reign of the Priest-King, setting the stage for sacramental participation in that reign.

7.5.3 Political Idolatry versus Allegiance to the Priest-King

Allegiance to Christ the Priest-King stands in stark contrast to political idolatry, where loyalty to nation or ideology eclipses loyalty to God's sovereign rule. Political idolatry manifests when citizens equate patriotism with devotion, turning flags and leaders into objects of worship rather than instruments of service. The Melchizedekian counter-model insists that ultimate allegiance belongs to the King of Salem—Christ—whose kingdom is "not of this world" (John 18:36). Jesus's warning that one cannot serve both God and money (Matt 6:24) extends to serving God and secular powers; loyalties must be prioritized. When political decisions conflict with Christ's ethical edicts—defending the poor, welcoming strangers, seeking peace—believers must obey the higher authority (Acts 5:29). This prophetic stance echoes Melchizedek's blessing of Abram in God Most High's name, signifying that God's claim supersedes all earthly sovereignties. The church's vocation then includes prophetic critique of imperial abuses, calling rulers to justice and humility. Nonviolent resistance and civil disobedience have biblical precedents—Shadrach, Meshach, and Abednego in Daniel 3—and resonate with a Melchizedekian ethic that refuses complicity in injustice. Allegiance to the Priest-King also frames political engagement as service rather than power acquisition: believers bring kingdom values into public office rather than seeking power's prestige. This posture elevates the common good over partisan gain and anticipates the harmony of the eschatological kingdom. Moving from ethics to liturgy, we next explore how Eucharistic continuity invites believers into direct participation in Christ's eternal priesthood.

7.6. Eucharistic Continuity: Bread, Wine, Body, Blood

7.6.1 From Salem's Table to the Upper Room (Luke 22:19–20)

 The bread-and-wine hospitality of Melchizedek finds its fullest echo in Jesus's Last Supper with His disciples, where He identifies Himself as the Living Bread and Eternal Wine. In Luke 22:19–20, Jesus takes unleavened bread—ritual of Passover—and gives it new meaning: "This is my body given for you." Similarly, the cup becomes "the new covenant in my blood," directly linking Salem's ancient meal to the new covenant sealed in Christ's sacrifice. This narrative shift transcends a singular event; it establishes an enduring sacrament that invites participation in the Melchizedekian priesthood. The location—a borrowed upper room—mirrors the temporary tent of Salem but signals the permanent tent of God's presence among humanity (Rev 21:3). The sequence of blessing, breaking, and sharing bread parallels Melchizedek's blessing of Abram, yet now the roles reverse: the priest-king becomes the sacrificial victim. The Eucharist thus becomes a memorial (*anamnesis*) that re-members Christ's once-for-all act while importing its power into the present. By gathering around this table, believers reenact the Salem covenant meal, transcending time and space. The disciples' initial failure to grasp the meal's full import underscores that full understanding emerges only with resurrection revelation (Luke 24:30–31). This liturgical continuity weaves Scripture's tapestry from Genesis through the Gospels, demanding that every Eucharistic celebration heed the ancient pattern fulfilled in Christ.

7.6.2 "Do This" as Participation in Eternal Priesthood (1 Corinthians 10:16)

When Jesus commands "Do this in remembrance of me," He entrusts the church with perpetuating His priestly ministry through sacramental action. Paul reiterates this in 1 Corinthians 10:16: "The cup of blessing that we bless… is a participation in the blood of Christ." This participation (*koinōnía*) extends beyond mere symbolism, signaling actual sharing in Christ's atoning work. Through the elements, the congregation enters the priest-king's heavenly liturgy, joining Melchizedek's eternal service at God's altar. The act consecrates individuals as living sacrifices (Rom 12:1) and unites them into one body (1 Cor 10:17), reflecting both priestly offering and royal unity. The ongoing "Do this" echoes Melchizedek's perpetual priesthood, embedding church life within Christ's unbroken ministry. Failure to observe this command risks severing the community from its spiritual lifeline, as Paul warns against unworthy reception (1 Cor

11:27–29). Ethical exhortations within Corinthians link eating and drinking the Lord's Supper to moral coherence—one cannot partake of Christ's body while living in division. Thus, participation in the Eucharist demands social reconciliation, aligning communal life with the priest-king's covenant of peace. By obeying "Do this," the church not only remembers but embodies the eternal sacrifice and reign of Christ.

7.6.3 Pastoral Implications: Assurance, Unity, Mission

The Eucharist serves as a primary locus of pastoral care, offering assurance of forgiveness as participants taste the covenant's terms (1 John 1:7). By standing before the same altar, diverse believers experience unity that transcends ethnic, economic, and social barriers, fulfilling Paul's vision in Galatians 3:28. This unity equips the church for mission, for a reconciled community becomes a credible sign to the world of God's reconciling power in Christ (2 Cor 5:18–20). Liturgical practices—common confession, shared cup, mutual blessing—encourage mutual accountability and sacrificial love. Pastors teach that the Eucharist is both a gift and a call: a gift of grace received and a call to "go and bear fruit that will last" (John 15:16). The table thus becomes a training ground for kingdom living, where reception of Christ's life empowers service and evangelism. Especially in contexts of conflict, the Eucharist models reconciliation, inviting former enemies to break bread together in peace. The sacrament's visceral elements—taste, smell, touch—imprint the reality of Christ's presence on the body, deepening faith beyond mere intellectual assent. By integrating doctrine, devotion, and deed, the Eucharist offers a comprehensive pastoral framework for sustaining believers under the Priest-King's reign.

7.7. Universal Mission: Jew and Gentile Gathered to One Priest-King

7.7.1 Ephesians 2:14–18 and the Breaking of Hostile Walls

Paul's vision in Ephesians 2:14–18 portrays Christ as our peace, breaking down the dividing wall of hostility between Jew and Gentile. This wall, originally a literal partition in Herod's Temple, becomes a metaphor for every barrier—ethnic, religious, social—that fragments humanity. In Christ's priestly-kingly work, reconciliation transcends former hostilities, creating one new humanity under God's one covenant (Eph 2:15). Through the cross, He abolishes enmity and unites both groups into a single body, offering access to the Father by one Spirit (Eph 2:18). This universal mission reflects Melchizedek's hospitality that extended beyond tribal boundaries—Abraham, a foreigner, received blessing (Gen 14:18). The church today continues this mission by tearing down walls of prejudice—racism, casteism, nationalism—inviting all into covenant fellowship. Missional strategies emerging from Ephesians include multiethnic congregations, intentional partnership between churches of different backgrounds, and corporate worship that honors diverse traditions. By embodying unity-in-diversity, the church testifies to the Priest-King's reconciling reign. This radical inclusion advances the gospel as a universal good, not a sectarian privilege. The breaking of hostile walls thus becomes the practical outworking of Melchizedekian hospitality on a global scale, preparing us to examine the Jerusalem Council's concrete outworking of this principle.

7.7.2 Acts 15 and the Jerusalem Council—Practical Outworking

The Jerusalem Council recorded in Acts 15 provides a case study of how the early church navigated Jewish-Gentile relations under the guidance of the Holy Spirit. Faced with disputes over circumcision and the Law, the apostles convened to discern God's will for Gentile believers. Peter's testimony—God gave the Holy Spirit to Gentiles as He did to Jews—echoes Melchizedek's universal priesthood, where no ethnic credential dictates inclusion. The council's decree, limiting Gentile obligations to essentials—abstaining from idolatry, blood, and sexual immorality—embodies a covenantal minimalism akin to Melchizedek's streamlined liturgy. By affirming Gentile full membership without imposing the entire Mosaic code, the church enacted Melchizedekian hospitality, welcoming outsiders into the family of faith. Barnabas and Paul's subsequent missionary journeys spread this inclusive model, planting communities where Jewish and Gentile believers shared in one table. The council's resolution prevented schism and established a precedent for resolving theological disputes through conciliar discernment. This practical outworking demonstrates that Melchizedek's archetype of open priesthood has tangible implications for church governance and mission strategy. The Jerusalem Council thus stands as a blueprint for reconciling tradition and innovation in pursuit of gospel unity. Building on this, we now consider missional hospitality as the church's ongoing enactment of Salem's peace.

7.7.3 Missional Hospitality: Extending Salem's Peace to the Nations

Missional hospitality enacts Melchizedek's legacy by offering Jesus-centered welcome to diverse peoples in their cultural contexts. Models such as relational evangelism, community development, and contextual liturgy ensure that the gospel resonates within local customs without compromising Christ's lordship. Churches partner with refugee agencies, open their doors to displaced families, and create intercultural worship services—tangible expressions of Melchizedek's covenant table. Language cafés, intercultural fellowships, and shared meals dismantle suspicions and build trust, reclaiming hospitality as a means of embodying peace. Missionaries, as modern Abram-like pioneers, often rely on local believers' hospitality, continuing the ancient rhythm of reciprocal blessing. Training programs emphasize cultural sensitivity, social justice, and power-sharing—principles aligned with Melchizedek's integrated office of justice and mercy. Digital platforms also facilitate missional hospitality by connecting global Christians in prayer and resource exchange. This expansive approach invites every believer into Christ's priestly-kingly mission: to proclaim, demonstrate, and embody the kingdom's peace. By weaving these practices into congregational life, the church avoids isolationism and participates in the global priesthood after Melchizedek's order. Having surveyed universal mission, we transition to the realm of spiritual warfare, where Christ's royal triumph secures victory.

7.8. Spiritual Warfare and Victorious Procession

7.8.1 The Cross as Royal Triumph (Colossians 2:15)

Colossians 2:15 proclaims that Christ disarmed the rulers and authorities, triumphing over them by the cross. This victory motif transforms the crucifixion into a royal procession, where the dying King-Priest parades defeated powers as spoils of His atoning work. The imagery recalls Roman triumphs, yet subverts them: instead of spoils of war, Christ's victory yields forgiveness, liberation, and reconciliation. By bearing the sin of the world, He exposed the tyranny of death and sin, demonstrating His authority over the most formidable foes (Heb 2:14–15). This triumphal theology positions the cross as the zenith of Melchizedekian kingship—merging priestly sacrifice with royal conquest. Believers, united to Christ, share in this triumph, living as overcomers even amid spiritual conflict (Rev 12:11). Worship of the cross thus becomes celebration of the King's coronation, where every demonic claim disintegrates before divine love. Liturgical observances of Good Friday and Easter Sunday commemorate and reenact this victory, grounding Christian hope in an invincible Priest-King. This royal triumph sets the stage for Psalm 110's prophecy of subjugation underfoot.

170

7.8.2 Psalm 110:1–2 and the Subjection of Enemies under Foot

Psalm 110:1–2 describes the Messiah's enthronement at God's right hand and His exercise of priestly-royal judgment: "The Lord will extend your mighty scepter from Zion; you will rule in the midst of your enemies… you will crush them with your rod of iron." This vivid imagery portrays the King-Priest subduing opposition, aligning with Colossians 2:15's triumph. Acts 2:34–35 and Hebrews 1:13 quote Psalm 110 to validate Christ's ascension and sovereignty, underscoring its christological import. The psalm's militaristic language—rod, scepter, footstool—melds royal and judicial symbols, capturing Melchizedek's dual office. In spiritual warfare, believers look to this prophecy as assurance that final victory belongs to the King-Priest. Preaching and teaching on Psalm 110 inspire confidence in facing personal and cosmic struggles, affirming that no power can ultimately overthrow God's reign. The church's mission then includes proclaiming this subjection, inviting all creation to acknowledge Christ's lordship. By embracing Psalm 110's imagery, the church grounds its spiritual battle in divine victory rather than human strategies. The transition to the practical outworking of this warfare emerges in the metaphor of the Armor of God.

7.8.3 Armor of God as Priestly-Royal Regalia (Ephesians 6:10–18)

Paul's description of the Armor of God in Ephesians 6:10–18 translates royal and priestly symbolism into daily spiritual combat gear. The belt of truth echoes the priestly girdle, securing the heart in covenant faithfulness. The breastplate of righteousness parallels Melchizedek's "king of righteousness," protecting the vital organs against accusations and guilt. The gospel of peace as shoes signifies readiness to advance the King's peacemaking mission. The shield of faith absorbs the fiery darts of the evil one, reflecting trust in the King-Priest's shield over His people. The helmet of salvation guards the mind, affirming the salvific reign inaugurated at the cross. The sword of the Spirit—God's word—embodies the royal decree that judges thoughts and hearts. Prayer in the Spirit sustains communion with the throne, echoing Melchizedek's perpetual intercession. This armor imagery integrates priestly and royal functions, demonstrating how believers participate in Christ's victory. Churches often teach these components as spiritual disciplines, equipping congregations to live courageously under the Priest-King's banner. By donning this regalia, Christians enter every arena—workplaces, homes, public squares—as ambassadors of a reign that conquers through righteousness and peace. Having explored spiritual warfare, we prepare to conclude by reflecting on ecclesial identity under the eternal Priest-King.

7.9. Ecclesial Identity: A Royal Priesthood after the Order

7.9.1 1 Peter 2:9 and Baptismal Consecration

1 Peter 2:9 declares that followers of Christ are "a chosen race, a royal priesthood, a holy nation, a people for God's own possession," consecrated by baptism into Messiah's eternal service. This baptismal consecration echoes Melchizedek's silent genealogy—believers derive their identity not from bloodlines but from Spirit-birth (John 3:5). Emerging from the waters, Christians symbolically die to old allegiances and rise as priests who intercede for the world (Rom 6:3–4). The designation "royal priesthood" unites kingly and priestly functions in every believer, reflecting Christ's dual office (Rev 1:6). Just as Melchizedek served as mediator between Abraham and El Elyon, baptized Christians mediate divine grace to their neighbors through prayer and deed. The lexical coupling of "royal" and "priesthood" in the same phrase underscores the inseparability of service and lordship in the church's calling. Baptism therefore is not a mere rite of admission but the act that imparts priest-king status, commissioning believers for worship and witness. Catechumens are taught that their new name signifies membership in a heavenly court, where they carry the King's

message to strangers and allies alike. The communal dimension of baptism—immersion in church fellowship—mirrors Salem's covenant meals, forging solidarity across social divides. As baptized priests, Christians bear responsibility to cultivate holiness, offering spiritual sacrifices of praise (Heb 13:15). This identity shifts ecclesial self-understanding from a cultural institution to a dynamic priestly-royal organism. The ongoing affirmation of baptismal vows at Easter and Pentecost renews this consecration, deepening communal roots in Christ's unending mediation. From this foundation, charisms and offices flow naturally, which we examine next.

7.9.2 Charisms and Offices—Gifts that Flow from the Ascended Priest-King

The outpouring of the Spirit at Pentecost (Acts 2:1–4) inaugurates the distribution of charisms—spiritual gifts such as teaching, healing, prophecy, and administration—empowering the church's priestly and kingly functions. These gifts derive from the ascended Priest-King who "gives gifts to men" (Eph 4:8). Apostles, prophets, evangelists, pastors, and teachers (Eph 4:11) constitute distinct offices that guide, protect, and equip the body. This apostolic-prophetic-pastoral framework parallels the tripartite structure of priest, prophet, and king, unified in Christ. Charisms such as hospitality and compassion extend Melchizedek's legacy of sacred welcome, while gifts of discernment preserve doctrinal purity. The exercise of gifts fosters communal flourishing, as each member contributes to the whole (1 Cor 12:4–7). Lay leadership enables the church to govern itself under Christ's authority, reflecting His royal rule through covenantal accountability. Deacons, rooted in service, mirror the priestly concern for the needy, administering practical care. Missionaries, as evangelistic prophets, proclaim the Gospel's reach to the nations, enacting the Pri-est-King's universal reign. Liturgical ministries—servers, musicians, readers—participate in heavenly worship (Rev 4:9–11), bringing earth into chorus with heaven. This charismatic ecosystem ensures that Christ's priest-kingly mission continues dynamically, not statically. By stewarding these gifts responsibly, the church embodies its identity as both a kingdom of priests and a royal assembly under the eternal High Priest.

7.9.3 Liturgy as Participation in Heavenly Ministry (Hebrews 12:22–24)

Hebrews 12:22–24 presents the church as enrolled in "Mount Zion, the city of the living God" where angels, the spirits of righteous men made perfect, Jesus the mediator of a new covenant, and the sprinkled blood unite in worship. Christian liturgy thus becomes participation in the heavenly liturgy presided over by Christ, the Melchizedekian Priest-King. Every element—scripture reading, sermon, prayers, sacraments—echoes the worship of the celestial court. Incense and chant recall angelic praise, while the Eucharist aligns earth's offering with the Lamb's unending sacrifice. Processions, vestments, and bells symbolize the regal and priestly dimensions of liturgical action. When the congregation proclaims the Sanctus ("Holy, holy, holy"), they join Seraphim around the heavenly throne (Isa 6:3). Liturgical calendars map Christ's salvific acts—incarnation, passion, resurrection, ascension—mirroring the celestial narrative. The spatial arrangement of church architecture—nave, sanctuary, altar—points toward the true Temple in heaven. The renewal of baptismal vows during Easter Vigil re-enacts entry into Christ's heavenly realm. Liturgical silence anticipates the eternal Sabbath rest promised to the priest-people (Heb 4:9–10). Through these practices, believers experience foretaste of the eschatological worship to come, where no veil separates them from the divine presence. Thus, liturgy functions not as mere commemoration but as active participation in Christ's ongoing ministry before the throne.

7.10. Eschatological Consummation— From Salem to New Jerusalem

7.10.1 Revelation 5:10 and Co-Reigning with the Lamb

Revelation 5:10 declares that Jesus has "made us a kingdom and priests to our God, and we shall reign on the earth," envisioning the faithful as co-regents under the Lamb. This co-reigning motif extends Melchizedek's priest-king paradigm into the eschaton, where the community of the redeemed shares corporate authority. This reign is not tyrannical but administered in justice, mercy, and peace, reflecting the character of the Priest-King. The sense of corporate kingship invites believers to steward creation responsibly, anticipating the new heavens and new earth (Rev 21:1). Co-reigning thus implies active participation in God's restorative project: healing creation, upholding righteousness, and sustaining worship. The priestly role continues as the people offer "harps and bowls of incense" representing "the prayers of the saints" (Rev 5:8). By co-reigning, the saints perpetuate Christ's priestly service on earth, manifesting the indissoluble unity of worship and rule. This vision empowers the church to anticipate kingdom realities in the present, aligning social action with eschatological hope. The co-reigning motif culminates in the New Jerusalem's descent, where priestly-royal offices dissolve into direct communion with God and the Lamb.

7.10.2 Marriage Supper of the Lamb as Ultimate Bread-and-Wine Feast

Revelation 19:9 describes the Marriage Supper of the Lamb—the ultimate covenant meal—where the Bride is invited to dine with Christ, her heavenly Spouse. This eschatological feast recapitulates Melchizedek's bread-and-wine archetype and Jesus's institution of the Eucharist. The marriage imagery invokes intimate union and joyful celebration, where every tear is wiped away (Rev 21:4). The Supper transcends ritual remembrance, becoming a participatory banquet of eternal life. The banquet hall, symbolizing the New Jerusalem, features "the river of the water of life" and "the tree of life" bearing healing leaves (Rev 22:1–2). Guests recline in perfect fellowship under the radiance of God's glory, no veil separating them. The Marriage Supper thus embodies consummated priest-king hospitality, where divine blessing overflows. Liturgical anticipations of this feast shape Advent and Easter themes, infusing worship with eschatological longing. Preachers draw on this vision to comfort the grieving and galvanize discipleship, reminding believers of their place at the heavenly banquet. The marriage sup better fuses covenantal fidelity with revelatory joy, sealing the church's identity as the Bride and fellowship of the Priest-King. As the narrative banquet closes, the end of mediated space unfolds in the final section.

7.10.3 God and the Lamb as Temple (Revelation 21:22)—End of Mediated Space

Revelation 21:22 proclaims that in the New Jerusalem, "I saw no temple in the city, for its temple is the Lord God the Almighty and the Lamb." This radical statement ends all spatial mediation: no altar or high priest is needed because divine presence fills every dimension. The union of God and the Lamb as Temple confirms that the Melchizedekian pattern—priesting and kinging—culminates in God Himself as both worshiper and worshiped. In this consummated reality, believers' priestly service becomes direct offering of praise, and royal rule manifests in unbroken fellowship with the divine presence. The end of mediated space invites reflection on sacramental practice: while liturgies anticipate this fullness, they remain provisional signs pointing beyond themselves. The absence of temple also dissolves denominational and geographical boundaries, uniting all redeemed in one homogenous worship. By ending physical mediation, Revelation fulfills Psalm 46:4's promise of God's dwelling "among His people," eliminating separation. The vision reinvigorates Christian hope, situating earthly mediations within the horizon of ultimate absence—where Christ, the true Temple, reigns unchallenged. This eschatological culmination provides a fitting close to the Priest-King's story, transitioning us to comparative theologies and dialogues in the next chapter.

7.11. Comparative Theologies and Contemporary Dialogues

7.11.1 Eastern and Western Liturgical Uses of Melchizedek

Eastern Orthodox anaphoras, such as those of St. Basil and St. John Chrysostom, explicitly reference Melchizedek's bread and wine offering as a prefiguration of Christ's sacrifice. In these rites, priests recite prayers likening the Eucharistic gifts to Melchizedek's mysterious offering, embedding Genesis 14 within the Eucharistic anamnesis. Western liturgies—from the Gallican to the Roman—include implicit Melchizedek allusions through Prefaces and collects that hail Christ as "priest forever after the order of Melchizedek." Medieval manuscript illumination often depicts Melchizedek alongside Abraham at the offertory table, reinforcing the archetype in visual catechesis. Post-Tridentine Missals standardized these references in the Roman Canon, while Protestant liturgies— Anglican, Lutheran—retain echoes in Scriptural Credences and Communion prayers. In contemporary liturgical renewal movements, theologians recover Melchizedek's typology to enrich interdenominational dialogue on Eucharistic theology. These liturgical uses demonstrate ecumenical convergences, as diverse traditions draw from the same biblical well. They also highlight variations in emphasis—Eastern rites often stress cosmic dimensions, Western ones focus on atonement. By studying these patterns, scholars and pastors gain insight into how Melchizedek's legacy shapes worship across Christian cultures. This comparative liturgical analysis sets the stage for examining doctrinal debates from the Reformation era.

7.11.2 Reformation Debates on Priesthood of All Believers

The Protestant Reformation's proclamation of the priesthood of all believers (1 Peter 2:9) revived Melchizedekian themes—namely, that Christ's priesthood abolished exclusive clerical mediation. Luther and Calvin rejected sacerdotal hierarchies, arguing that every baptized Christian shares in Christ's royal priesthood. This democratization of priestly status sparked controversies over lay communion, private confession, and church governance. Anglicans responded with via media solutions, retaining ordained ministry while affirming universal priesthood. Radical Reformers like the Anabaptists extended priesthood to communal discernment of gifts, emphasizing charisms over offices. By grounding Reform theology in Melchizedek's archetype rather than Aaronic exclusivity, Reformers reoriented ecclesiology toward direct access to God. These debates shaped doctrinal formulations in confessions and catechisms, influencing modern Protestant denominations. Contemporary discussions on ordination, women's ministry, and LGBTQ inclusion trace their roots to Reformation convictions about priesthood. Revisiting Melchizedek's example aids these dialogues, reminding the church of its foundational calling to priestly mediation without clerical monopoly. Understanding Reformation history thus enriches present conversations on authority, ministry, and lay participation.

7.11.3 Interfaith Perspectives: Judaism, Islam, and Modern Spirituality

In Jewish thought, Melchizedek appears in rabbinic midrash as a symbol of righteous non-Israelite worship, informing contemporary Jewish-Christian dialogue on shared biblical heritage. Some Islamic traditions analogize Melchizedek's "priest of God Most High" with Islamic concepts of tawhīd and righteous rule (*mulk*), offering points of contact in interfaith discussions. New Age and esoteric movements often appropriate Melchizedek as an "Ascended Master," reflecting a syncretistic spirituality that posits universal archetypes beyond doctrinal boundaries. While these appropriations diverge significantly from biblical witness, they underscore Melchizedek's archetypal power in global imagination. Interfaith dialogues can use Melchizedek's figure as a starting point to explore themes of divine mediation, ethical leadership, and spiritual hospitality. Such conversations must tread carefully, distinguishing authentic theological insights from syncretistic readings. By acknowledging Melchizedek's multifaceted reception, Christian theologians can engage respectfully with other faith perspectives while clarifying the distinctiveness of Christ's fulfillment. This interfaith engagement enriches Christian self-understanding, sharpening appreciation for the depth and uniqueness of Melchizedek's revelation in Scripture. As the church navigates pluralistic contexts, Melchizedek's story invites conversations about shared values and redemptive uniqueness, concluding our comparative survey.

Conclusion

In Christ, the priestly blessing and royal scepter that Melchizedek once held apart now find perfect union and eternal outworking. The bread and wine of Salem's ancient table become living symbols of a covenant sealed once for all, and the quiet court of that Canaanite king anticipates the global assembly under the risen Son's rule. Through His death and resurrection, Jesus fulfills every promise implicit in Melchizedek's order, inaugurating a reign of justice, mercy, and peace that knows no end. As we move into the practical dimensions of life under this eternal Priest-King, we carry forward both the weight of ancient mystery and the hope of final consummation.

Chapter 8: Liturgical and Devotional Legacy

Liturgy and devotion form the twin arteries through which the life of Melchizedek continues to pulse within the body of Christ. From the earliest gatherings in private homes and catacombs to the soaring grandeur of basilicas and contemporary living rooms, Christian worship has preserved the theology of the eternal Priest-King in ritual, word, and song. Each gesture— the breaking of bread, the lifting of incense, the sung psalm— carries forward an ancient memory of Salem's hospitality and the heavenly liturgy that Melchizedek foreshadowed. Devotional practices, whether structured or spontaneous, invite believers into an encounter with the same divine presence that once greeted Abraham. As the church's calendar unfolds year by year, these patterns of prayer and praise shape not only what we believe but how we live, infusing daily rhythms with echoes of the eschatological feast to come. In exploring the liturgical and devotional legacy of Melchizedek, we uncover the ways worship anchors theology in the body, mind, and heart, ensuring that the mystery of the Priest-King remains both remembered and realized.

8.1. Introduction: Sacred Memory in Action

8.1.1 Why Liturgy Preserves Theology

Liturgy functions as theology enacted: every gesture, word, and symbol in corporate worship embodies and communicates core doctrinal truths. When Melchizedek brought bread and wine to Abraham (Genesis 14:18–20), he enacted a theologically rich moment that the church now re-members in the Eucharist. By repeating ritual actions—blessing bread, pouring wine—the liturgy teaches that Christ's once-for-all sacrifice undergirds all ongoing worship (Hebrews 10:10). The Psalms, which informed ancient temple worship (Psalm 100), continue to shape psalm-centric liturgies, reinforcing themes of divine kingship and priestly intercession. Liturgical phrases like "Holy, holy, holy" (Isaiah 6:3; Revelation 4:8) embed cosmic worship language in Christian rites, reminding believers that earthly worship participates in heaven's praise. When congregations recite the Creed, they confess historical events—incarnation, passion, resurrection—as divine realities shaping present faith. The pattern of readings from Torah, Prophets, and Epistles mirrors canonical structure, preserving the unified witness of Scripture. Vestments and architecture—altars, fonts, tabernacles—embody theological convictions about Christ's sacramental presence among His people. Incense and bells, inherited from temple practice, signify prayer rising to heaven and the king's royal court. In liturgical action, theology becomes tangible, bridging the gap between abstract doctrine and embodied faith. Over centuries, this preservation has guarded orthodoxy against theological drift, because communities literally "do what they believe." Liturgical calendars, marking Advent, Lent, Easter, situate the gospel in time, ensuring that each season underscores Christ's priestly, kingly, and prophetic roles. By safeguarding theology within repeated sacred forms, liturgy becomes both teacher and guardrail, embedding Melchizedek's archetype within the church's DNA. This liturgical function naturally leads into the devotional heart of worship, where private devotion animates public rites.

8.1.2 Devotion as the Heart's Liturgy

While corporate liturgy structures communal worship, private devotion enlivens the soul's personal encounter with the Priest-King. Early Christians practiced *lectio divina*, reading Scripture meditatively to hear Christ's voice, an echo of Melchizedek's silent yet powerful presence in Genesis. Prayer disciplines—morning and evening prayers—establish daily rhythms that sanctify time, as the church prays "Lord, you have been our dwelling place in all generations" (Psalm 90:1). Fasting, drawn from botanical metaphors in Isaiah 58, deepens hunger for divine justice and mercy, mirroring Melchizedek's combined emphasis on righteousness and peace. The Jesus Prayer—"Lord Jesus Christ, Son of God, have mercy on me, a sinner"—functions as a personal invocation of priestly intercession, rehearsing Christ's eternal advocacy (1 John 2:1). Devotional psalmody, through repeated chanting of Psalms 23 and 51, fosters interior renewal and trust in the Shepherd-King. Icon veneration in the East serves as a window to heaven, inviting contemplative devotion that transcends words. Rosary beads in the Western tradition guide meditation on gospel events, integrating Christ's incarnational mystery into daily life. Journaling and spiritual diaries record divine encounters, discerning the Holy Spirit's movement in personal history. Hymn singing in private settings—Charles Wesley's "And Can It Be?"—affirms Christ's priestly solidarity with sinners (Hebrews 4:15). Silence and solitude, following Jesus's precedent of withdrawing to pray (Mark 1:35), create space for the soul's reconciliation with God's presence. Devotional theology thus personalizes liturgical truths, ensuring that ritual forms find resonance in individual hearts. Together, liturgy and devotion form complementary pathways into the same divine reality, preparing us to trace these patterns back to their apostolic origins.

8.2. Apostolic Roots: From Upper Room to Catacombs

8.2.1 The Didache and First-Century Table Rites

The *Didache*, an early Christian manual dating to the late first century, preserves one of the earliest Eucharistic prayers after the Lord's Supper, illustrating how apostolic communities framed their table rites. It instructs believers to give thanks "after this manner" for the cup and the broken bread, echoing Jesus's own formulas (Luke 22:19–20). The *Didache* also connects the meal to initiatives of charity, directing that itinerant prophets and teachers be received as the Lord, for in doing so, one serves Christ (Didache 11:5). This intertwining of hospitality with sacrament parallels Melchizedek's hospitality to Abraham, where political courtesy became covenantal celebration. Baptism preceded Eucharist in the *Didache* (Didache 7–9), reinforcing the order of initiation and meal, similar to the pattern of washings and laying on of hands in Hebrews 6:1–2. The community's communal meal emphasized unity, with admonitions against division and gluttony (Didache 14:1–3). These table rites, often celebrated in private homes, fostered intimacy and theological teaching in one setting. The *Didache*'s eucharistic thanksgiving concludes with prayers for deliverance from sin and the coming kingdom—a direct link to eschatological hope (Matthew 6:10). By studying this document, we glimpse how Melchizedek's archetype shaped the earliest Christian worship, blending covenant meal, prophecy, and communal solidarity. This apostolic practice in turn informed later liturgical development, as the church spread beyond Judea, leaving a tangible legacy in catacomb art and funerary piety.

8.2.2 Catacomb Frescoes, Eucharistic Symbol, and Martyr Piety

Beneath the streets of Rome, catacomb frescoes from the second and third centuries depict scenes of fish, loaves, and the Good Shepherd—visual shorthand for the Eucharist. The

183

fish (**Ichthys**) symbol, an acronym for "Jesus Christ, God's Son, Savior," appears alongside loaves in chamber walls, indicating commemorations of the Lord's Supper in proximity to burial places. These images affirm that even amid persecution, believers gathered to celebrate the sacrament in contexts of martyrdom, trusting in Christ's promise to meet them "where two or three are gathered" (Matthew 18:20). Tomb inscriptions—"In peace I sleep, awaiting the resurrection"—link funerary hope to baptism and Eucharist, reinforcing the Melchizedekian theme of death's defeat. Martyr accounts, such as those of Perpetua and Felicity, describe visions of the heavenly banquet following their sacrifice, demonstrating the seamless connection between earthly rites and anticipated eschatological feast. Archeological evidence shows small arched recesses (cubicula) where families gathered for agape meals before interring their dead. Pottery fragments bearing the sign of the chalice and bread confirm that the Eucharist transcended liturgical centers, becoming integral to daily faith even at the threshold of death. These catacomb practices preserved the theology of Melchizedek's eternal priesthood: even as bodies decayed, the living Priest-King interceded before the Father. In this subterranean worship, the community enacted hope, worship, and unity, underlining that Christian identity was rooted in the Melchizedekian table rather than empire's halls. The transition from these secret rites to dominant liturgical expressions unfolds in the next chapter.

8.3. Byzantine Radiance: Heavenly Worship on Earth

8.3.1 The Anaphoras of St. Basil and St. John Chrysostom

The Byzantine rite preserves two primary Eucharistic prayers: the Anaphora of St. Basil and that of St. John Chrysostom. Both include explicit references to Melchizedek's offering: the priest invokes how Melchizedek "brought forth bread and wine to Abraham our father, King of Salem and priest of the Most

High God." This biblical recall anchors Christian worship in the ancient covenant meal, affirming continuity with Melchizedek's archetype. The anaphoras proceed through Trinitarian praise, recitation of salvation history, epiclesis (invocation of the Holy Spirit), and thanksgiving, reflecting the cosmic scope of divine liturgy portrayed in Revelation 4–5. In the epiclesis, the celebrant prays that the bread and wine become the body and blood of Christ—linking earthly elements to heavenly reality. The rich theological language—terms like *anamnesis*, *eucharistia*, and *doxology*—weaves Scripture with patristic interpretation, ensuring that each word conveys layered meaning. Incense, carrying symbolic smoke of offering, blends with chants of "Holy" from Isaiah 6:3 and Revelation 4:8, transporting worshipers into the celestial throne room. Byzantine hymnography—Cherubic hymn, Trisagion—structures musical theology, inviting congregants to join angels in unending praise. Through these anaphoras, the church experiences a foretaste of heavenly worship, participating in Melchizedek's eternal service. The rhythmic repetition of these prayers shapes communal memory and personal devotion, forging a distinctive beatitude of the soul. Transitioning from liturgical form to visual theology, we next consider the role of icons and incense.

8.3.2 Icons, Incense, and the Cosmic Vision of Divine Liturgy

Icons in Orthodox worship function as "windows to heaven," allowing the faithful to enter the divine realm through sight. Images of Christ Pantocrator reign in the sanctuary, while icons of Melchizedek blessing Abraham appear in some traditions, linking Old Testament worship to its fulfillment. The ritual use of incense, following Psalm 141:2 ("Let my prayer be counted as incense before you"), signifies the prayers of saints ascending before the throne. In tandem with icon veneration, incense frames the entire liturgy as participation in the cosmic worship described in Revelation. Processions with chandeliers and incense reverberate melismatic chants, symbolizing the movement of the Spirit in creation. The spatial arrangement of the iconostasis—separating nave and sanctuary—represents the intersection of earth and heaven, the very meeting point Melchizedek foreshadowed. Worshipers light tapers before icons, enacting the priestly offering of light, recalling that the King-Priest is "light of the world" (John 8:12). Through these sensory elements—color, scent, chant—the Byzantine liturgy embodies theological truths about divine presence and human response. The cosmic vision of divine liturgy thus emerges as a multilayered enactment of salvation history, begun in Salem, perfected in Christ, and continually renewed in every eucharistic celebration. As this radiant worship flourishes in the East, the Latin West cultivates complementary syntheses of chant and chantiture, which we now explore.

8.4. Latin West: The Gregorian Synthesis

8.4.1 Roman Canon, Offertory Processions, and Chant

The Gregorian Sacramentary, compiled under Pope Gregory the Great, crystallized the Roman Canon—the Eucharistic prayer central to Western Latin liturgy. Its prayers recall Melchizedek's offering implicitly through thanksgiving for Christ's body and blood, described as "the living bread which came down from heaven" (John 6:51). The Offertory procession, introduced in the fourth century, saw bread and wine brought forward with solemn chant, symbolizing the royal priesthood's bringing of first fruits. Gregorian chant—monophonic, unmetered melodic lines—creates a timeless soundscape, suspending earthly time and evoking the heavenly liturgy. Texts like "Adoro te devote" and sequences such as "Victimae paschali laudes" blend scriptural references with doctrinal homilies, teaching the faithful through melody. The Council of Trent reaffirmed the primacy of the Roman Canon, preserving its textual integrity against liturgical variation. Medieval theological commentary—by Rupert of Deutz and Berengar of Tours—explicated how the Roman Canon fulfills sacrificial typology rooted in Melchizedek.

Architectural features—Roman basilicas with raised presbyteria—reflect the elevated role of the priest, echoing the high-place setting of Genesis 14. The Western emphasis on text and chant complements the Eastern icon-incense interplay, demonstrating two complementary expressions of the same Melchizedekian heritage. This liturgical corpus shaped the devotional life of medieval Europe, leading into the monastic hours discussed next.

8.4.2 Monastic Hours, Scholastic Commentary, and Popular Piety

Benedictine monasteries structured daily life around the Divine Office: eight canonical hours drawn from Psalms and canticles, sanctifying each segment of the day (Psalm 119:164). These hour services—Matins, Lauds, Prime through Compline—created a rhythmic sanctification of time, anticipating Melchizedek's unified priest-king rule over the calendar. Scholastic theologians like Thomas Aquinas composed hymns (e.g., "Adoro te devote") and theological treatises explaining sacramental presence, drawing on Melchizedek's archetype to teach Eucharistic theology. Popular piety flourished in lay confraternities that recited the Little Office of the Blessed Virgin, chanted the rosary, and processed relics, embedding liturgical forms into daily life. Pilgrims on the Camino de Santiago sang chant fragments and recited psalms, turning travel into a walking office of prayer. Guilds adopted patronal feasts—bakers honoring St. Lawrence, whose last meal echoes the Eucharistic banquet—connecting vocational life with liturgical calendar. Medieval drama—mystery and miracle plays—enacted biblical scenes, bringing Scripture's Melchizedekian moments to public squares. Lay confraternities maintained chapels and commissioned altarpieces depicting Melchizedek's offering, perpetuating his memory in parish contexts. This interplay of monastic structure, scholastic teaching, and popular devotion ensured that Melchizedek's liturgical legacy permeated every layer of medieval society. As the Reformation dawned, these unified forms gave way to vernacular refrains, which we will examine in Chapter 8.5.

8.5. Reform, Renewal, and Vernacular Refrains

8.5.1 Calvin, Cranmer, and the Shape of Reformed Worship

The Reformation ushered in a return to Scripture as the norm for worship, discarding medieval accretions that obscured the simplicity of the gospel (2 Timothy 3:16). John Calvin emphasized the primacy of preaching and congregational singing, arguing that the Word of God read and proclaimed should shape every aspect of the service. In Geneva, he instituted psalmody in the vernacular, replacing Latin chants with metrical Psalms so that laypeople could join heart and voice (Ephesians 5:19). Thomas Cranmer's Book of Common Prayer similarly streamlined the liturgy, translating key prayers into English and crafting the Eucharistic rite to highlight Christ's command "Do this in remembrance of me" (Luke 22:19). Cranmer's litany and collects prioritized biblical language, making theology accessible without sacrificing depth. Both Reformers rejected the notion of priests as a separate caste, instead reaffirming the priesthood of all believers (1 Peter 2:9) by seating ministers among the congregation. Architecture followed suit, with Reformed churches favoring plainer spaces and central pulpits to signify the authority of the Word. In these contexts, Melchizedek's archetype found new expression: the gift of bread and wine remained central but was understood as a sign pointing directly to Christ's singular sacrifice rather than a repeated propitiation. The Regulative Principle adopted by many Reformed bodies insisted that only elements commanded or exemplified in Scripture be retained, keeping the liturgy tethered to biblical warrant (Deuteronomy 12:32). As a result, Reformed worship became a distinctive blend of solemn order and heartfelt participation, echoing Melchizedek's blend of royal dignity and priestly simplicity. This shift laid the groundwork for later devotional movements that infused personal piety into corporate worship.

8.5.2 Pietist Devotions and the Hymnody Explosion

In the late seventeenth and eighteenth centuries, Pietism arose as a revival movement within Lutheranism emphasizing personal devotion and holy living over mere ritual observance. Philipp Jakob Spener's *Pia Desideria* called for small groups (*collegia pietatis*) that practiced prayer, Bible study, and mutual exhortation—an echo of Melchizedek's intimate covenant meal with Abraham, now replicated in communal gatherings. These groups fostered spontaneous expression of faith, leading to a surge of hymn writing that gave voice to private devotion in public worship. Hymnists like Paul Gerhardt and later Charles Wesley composed verses rich in Melchizedekian themes—Christ as the perfect priest offering His body and blood, the soul's deep hunger for righteousness and peace (Psalm 42:1). Wesley's hymns, in particular, wove theological depth with emotional warmth, inviting entire congregations to articulate their personal encounter with the Priest-King. The Methodist movement's camp meetings further democratized worship, as large gatherings sang hymns by the thousands, reciting lines about Christ's priestly advocacy and kingship over the heart. These devotional streams broadened the church's musical repertoire, moving beyond metrical Psalms to texts that drew from Scripture and experiential theology. Liturgically, many denominations incorporated new hymnals alongside traditional chant, creating a rich tapestry of song that invited both head and heart into worship. Pietist hymnody also inspired missionary work, with choruses translating into multiple languages and carrying Melchizedekian motifs to distant lands. This explosion of devotional music ensured that every believer could internalize the narrative of Christ's priest-king ministry through melody and meter, bridging the gap between liturgy and daily life.

8.6. Sacramental Theology: Signs That Work

8.6.1 Baptismal Mystagogy and Christian Identity

Baptism, rooted in the symbolic washings of the Old Covenant (Hebrews 6:2), took new shape in early church mystagogy, moving from catechumen instruction to post-baptismal reflection. As neophytes emerged from the water, they entered not simply a community but participated in Christ's death and resurrection (Romans 6:4), embodying the Melchizedekian pattern of priestly initiation beyond genealogy. Mystagogues taught the newly baptized that their identity now rested in Christ's eternal priesthood, marked by the sign of the cross and the oil of chrism—symbols of royal anointing and Spirit-empowerment (1 Samuel 16:13). Liturgical rites like the *Mystagogical Sermons* of Cyril of Jerusalem unpacked baptismal elements—water, white garment, and communion—revealing layers of typology linked to Melchizedek's bread and wine. The white garment symbolized participation in Christ's sinless priesthood; the chrism invoked Isaiah 61:1's anointing of the Messiah; and partaking of Eucharist immediately after baptism sealed the covenant. Over time, Western rites developed the *Rite of Baptism for Children*, emphasizing parental vows and godparent sponsorship, connecting individual initiation to communal intercession—an echo of Abram's tithing and covenant with Melchizedek. Contemporary liturgies continue these traditions, often including baptized candidates in the Eucharist and prayers for their growth into Christ's Melchizedekian priesthood. By approaching baptism as mystagogy, the church preserves sacramental theology as an experiential journey rather than a mere proclamation, anchoring Christian identity in the ongoing reality of the eternal Priest-King.

8.6.2 Eucharistic Presence—Real, Spiritual, Memorial

Debates over Eucharistic presence—whether Christ is present *in, with, and under* the elements (real presence), spiritually received by faith (reformed view), or remembered as a memorial (Zwinglian view)—all circle back to Melchizedek's offering of bread and wine. The Catholic medieval doctrine of transubstantiation, formalized at the Fourth Lateran Council (1215), holds that the substance of bread and wine become Christ's body and blood, affirming a continuous link between ritual and reality akin to Melchizedek's consecrated elements. Lutherans articulate *sacramental union*, affirming a real presence without metaphysical change, preserving both divine mystery and scriptural imagery (John 6:51). Reformed theologians emphasize the Spirit's agency in lifting the believer to commune with Christ, drawing on Hebrews 10:19–22's invitation to enter the heavenly sanctuary. Anabaptist traditions often highlight the Eucharist as a communal memorial and sign of covenant faithfulness, echoing Abraham's trust in Melchizedek's blessing. Contemporary ecumenical dialogues, such as the Lutheran-Catholic agreement on justification, seek common ground on sacramental presence, recognizing that divergent theological languages nevertheless point to the same Melchizedekian reality. The Anglican via media similarly holds a *real spiritual* presence, inviting both Catholic and Protestant to find unity in the mystery. Beyond doctrine, the practice of retreat liturgies and eucharistic adoration employs prayers and chants—such as the Tantum Ergo—emphasizing Christ's perpetual presence. This rich tapestry of sacramental theology ensures that the bread and wine remain living points of contact with the eternal Priest-King, shaping devotion and doctrine in tandem.

8.7. Daily Prayer: The Rhythm of Sanctified Time

8.7.1 Liturgy of the Hours, Divine Office, and Psalmody Cycles

The monastic *Liturgy of the Hours*, codified by the Rule of St. Benedict, established a framework for sanctifying every portion of the day with prayer, drawing heavily on the Psalms. By praying the *Opens* (Lauds) at dawn and the *Close* (Compline) at night, monks enacted a continuous offering of praise that mirrored Melchizedek's perpetual priesthood "without end of days" (Hebrews 7:3). The cycle of psalmody—150 Psalms distributed across the week—ensured that the full spectrum of human emotion and divine praise shaped the rhythm of prayer. The chanting of Psalms 118 and 136, with their refrains of God's steadfast love, reminded communities of covenant faithfulness. Over centuries, cathedral choirs and parish clergy adopted simplified versions of the Office, integrating psalmody into daily parishes and artisan guilds. The Divine Office became a shared discipline among both laity and clergy during medieval Europe, reinforcing a society oriented toward prayer. The structure of Matins, Lauds, Prime, Terce, Sext, None, Vespers, and Compline created spiritual landmarks, sanctifying work hours with interludes of divine praise. In the East, the *Horologion* adapted these hours, using prostrations and *kathismata* to deepen bodily participation. These daily prayers function as an ongoing liturgy in microcosm, embedding the ethos of Melchizedek's eternal service into every waking hour. The next subsection will examine how modern innovations bring this ancient rhythm into contemporary life.

8.7.2 Modern Breviaries, Prayer Apps, and Lay Participation

In response to post-Vatican II calls for the laity's fuller participation, publishers released affordable breviaries containing simplified offices, encouraging families and small groups to pray the Hours. Digital platforms and mobile apps—such as iBreviary and DivineOffice—offer daily psalm cycles, antiphons, and collects, making the ancient office accessible to commuters and remote workers. Push notifications remind users to "pray without ceasing" (1 Thessalonians 5:17), fostering communal rhythm even in fragmented schedules. Online prayer communities connect around the Hours via social media and video streaming, ensuring that Melchizedek's perpetual priesthood extends into digital space. Lay formation programs equip believers to lead and participate in short prayer services at workplaces, schools, and hospitals, demonstrating that liturgy transcends church buildings. Graphic designers adapt ancient psalm texts into visually engaging layouts for screens, honoring the aesthetic tradition of illuminated manuscripts. Podcasts and YouTube channels provide guided recitations, blending chant, instrumental music, and reflective commentary. These innovations democratize daily prayer, dissolving barriers of clergy-lay divide and geographical distance. As individuals chant Psalms 121 ("I lift up my eyes to the hills…") on their smartphones, they join a global chorus spanning centuries. This fusion of tradition and technology ensures that the liturgy of the hours remains a living practice, continuously renewing the church's Melchizedekian worship on earth.

8.8. Devotional Streams: Personalizing the Priest-King

8.8.1 Lectio Divina and Contemplative Encounter

Lectio Divina, a four-fold method of reading, meditation, prayer, and contemplation, invites the soul into an experiential encounter with Scripture, akin to Abraham's listening to Melchizedek's blessing. By reading a biblical passage slowly (*lectio*), the reader discerns a word or phrase that resonates. Meditation (*meditatio*) then probes its meaning, asking how Christ's priestly mediation speaks into one's life. Prayer (*oratio*) responds with personal dialogue, echoing Jesus's invitation to call Him "Abba" (Romans 8:15). Finally, contemplation (*contemplatio*) rests in God's presence without words, akin to standing before the unspoken majesty of the Priest-King. Monastic traditions, particularly in the Benedictine and Carthusian orders, have practiced *Lectio Divina* as the heart of communal life. Modern retreats and spiritual formation courses integrate this method into parish life, training laypeople to cultivate silent listening. Retreat centers offer guided sessions where participants experience the shift from reading about Christ to being with Christ. Digital tools—like audio scripture apps—enable *Lectio Divina* on the go, though practitioners caution against losing the contemplative stillness to multimedia distraction. Through *Lectio*, the Priest-King's word becomes an immediate encounter, personalizing the ancient archetype in the believer's daily rhythm.

8.8.2 Intercession, Healing Prayer, and Charismatic Gifts

The early church's life in Acts 4:29–30 demonstrates how urgent intercession unleashes divine power, modeling Melchizedek's priestly advocacy. Spiritual warfare and healing prayer ministries draw on this legacy, inviting the Holy Spirit to bring holistic restoration—body, soul, and spirit. Laying on of hands, an apostolic practice (Acts 8:17; 19:6), conveys blessing and empowerment, reflecting the priestly transfer of covenant life. Charismatic gifts—discernment, tongues, prophecy—function as tools for building up the body (1 Corinthians 12:7), just as Melchizedek served the faithful through blessing and mediation. Healing services often incorporate confession, anointing with oil, and communal prayer, aligning with James 5:14–15's instruction for the sick. Urban prayer gatherings use intercession maps to cover entire neighborhoods, enacting priestly presence in social space. Retreats dedicated to healing prayer bring counselors, worship leaders, and intercessors together, creating layered spaces of care. Practices of corporate lament, drawing on the Psalms, enable communities to engage collective pain before God, invoking both justice and mercy. This devotional stream highlights the continuing relevance of Melchizedek's priestly ministry in addressing physical and spiritual needs. As believers intercede and minister healing, they step into the archetypal role of Priest-King's agents, bridging heaven and earth through compassionate service.

8.9. Hymns, Psalms, and Spiritual Songs

8.9.1 Psalmody through the Ages—From Synagogue to Cathedral

The practice of psalm singing originates in the Jewish temple, where Levites chanted the five books of Davidic Psalms during daily sacrifices (1 Chronicles 16:7–36). By the second century A.D., early Christians adopted Psalm 23 ("The Lord is my shepherd") as a baptismal hymn, linking Melchizedek's bread-and-wine hospitality to Christ's shepherding care. In medieval monasteries, psalm cycles structured the Divine Office, ensuring that each psalm at least once a week infused monastic life with biblical prayer (Psalm 119:164). Gregorian chant preserved the original Latin texts, allowing monastic communities to dwell on the psalms' theological depth through melismatic melody. The Reformation's vernacular movements—e.g., the Genevan Psalter—translated psalms into French metre, enabling congregational singing and theological formation through Psalm 51's penitential pleas. In Anglican tradition, the Book of Common Prayer maintained psalmody at Morning and Evening Prayer, reinforcing communal identity around God's Word. Pietists turned to psalm paraphrases by Paul Gerhardt, setting refined theology to heartfelt melody. In the 20th century, Taizé introduced repetitive chant settings of psalms, fostering meditative worship across linguistic barriers. Contemporary churches blend ancient psalms with modern arrangements, using Psalm 100 in gospel, rock, or jazz styles to proclaim "Make a joyful noise to the Lord" in culturally relevant idioms. Digital hymnals and streaming services now index psalm settings by theme—comfort, lament, praise—so worshipers can select Psalm 46 ("God is our refuge") in times of crisis. This psalmody through the ages demonstrates the church's fidelity to scriptural praise while adapting forms to diverse contexts, preparing us to examine global worship music's vibrant expansions.

8.9.2 Global Worship Music, Indigenous Styles, and Digital Platforms

Since the late 20th century, global worship movements have integrated indigenous musical styles—African drumming in Ghana's "Oye Ohene" (Psalm 95), Indian Carnatic chants in Tamil psalm translations, and Native American flute underlays for Psalm 19's cosmic themes. This contextualization honors local cultures while proclaiming the universality of Melchizedek's hospitality, extending ritual welcome across ethnic divides (Ephesians 2:14–18). Global hymnwriters like Graham Kendrick have composed tunes that lend themselves to Gaelic, Swahili, and Vietnamese lyrics, ensuring that Revelation 5:9's "Worthy is the Lamb" resonates in every tongue. Digital platforms—YouTube, Spotify, church apps—disseminate these worship songs instantly, enabling small house churches in remote regions to access the latest freely licensed tracks. Collaborative platforms like SongSelect allow local worship leaders to translate and re-arrange popular worship anthems, marrying corporate authorship with indigenous creativity. Live streaming of international worship nights—Hillsong Conference, Passion—fosters a global liturgical solidarity, as thousands engage the same songs in different time zones. Virtual choirs like Eric Whitacre's advocate for remote participation, layering voices from diverse continents into unified praise. Worship technology integrates lyric projection and interactive lighting, creating multisensory experiences that echo early church's use of architecture and iconography. The spread of Afrocentric gospel choirs in urban megachurches brings Psalm 150's "praise him with tambourine and dance" into contemporary contexts. This global worship music movement exemplifies how devotion adapts to new media, prompting us next to consider how sacred spaces shape liturgical imagination.

Conclusion

The ongoing evolution of Christian worship—from its Judaic roots through medieval chant to twenty-first-century digital gatherings—demonstrates the enduring power of liturgy to transmit Melchizedek's archetype across cultures and eras. Every adaptation, whether ancient or novel, testifies that the church's highest calling is to rehearse the heavenly reality in concrete, embodied form. In this sacred choreography, believers are both participants and priests, offering spiritual sacrifices of praise (Heb 13:15) while proclaiming the unending reign of Christ, our Melchizedekian High Priest. As devotional practices draw the rhythms of prayer into everyday life—through breath prayers, lectio divina, or shared hymnody—they transform time itself into a sanctified gift, pointing beyond the present toward the Lamb's eternal banquet.

Ultimately, liturgy and devotion are more than pious exercises; they are eschatological signposts and social imaginaries, training the church to live as a foretaste of New Jerusalem. By weaving together word, sacrament, and song, the faithful enact the covenant hospitality that Melchizedek first modeled, offering a foretaste of the communion and peace that Christ secures for all creation. As we prepare to enter praxis—practicing Salem's peace in a fractured world—we carry forward this liturgical inheritance, confident that every act of worship, large or small, bears witness to the unshakable hope of the eternal Priest-King.

Chapter 9: Living in the Order of Melchizedek Today

To live "in the order of Melchizedek" today means to step into the vocation of both priest and king, not as an elite class but as every believer called to offer spiritual sacrifices and to advance God's reign in daily life. This chapter reframes Christian identity away from consumer Christianity toward covenantal belonging, grounding us in baptismal initiation and the timeless pattern of bread and wine. It unfolds how our routines—from moments of prayer at dawn to acts of justice in the public square—become liturgical gestures echoing Salem's day-long worship. Work, hospitality, finances, and advocacy are recast as sacred duties, each infused with the Melchizedekian blend of righteousness and peace. Whether you lead a board meeting, host a simple meal, or engage in digital discernment, you embody the cosmic liturgy inaugurated by the eternal Priest-King. By adopting rhythms of attention, generosity, and intercession, you align earthly vocation with heavenly service, inviting the world to taste God's kingdom here and now (Romans 12:1–2; Hebrews 7:3).

9.1. Re-Framing Identity: From Consumer to Royal Priest

9.1.1 Baptismal DNA and the Everyday Altar

Your baptism embeds you in Christ's eternal priesthood, marking you with divine identity rather than consumer choice. Emerging from the waters signifies death to self-centered living and resurrection into a priestly calling (Romans 6:4). Each morning, as you recall your baptismal vows, you reenact the laying down of old allegiances and the taking up of a daily altar of life experience. Your hands become vessels for offering spiritual sacrifices—acts of kindness, words of blessing—that the Scriptures call "acceptable to God" (1 Peter 2:5). This altar need not be built of stone; it can be the workspace where you speak truth in love or the commutes where you pray for your neighbors. Recognizing every moment as sacramental challenges the "consumer" mindset that treats faith as a product to acquire rather than a vocation to embody. You cease to ask, "What does the church do for me?" and begin to ask, "How may I serve as priest in my context?" This shift in posture transforms routine tasks— emails, errands, meals—into liturgical acts offered to the King. As you bless your family at the breakfast table or pray for colleagues in the office, you practice priest-king holiness in miniature. Sunday worship then becomes the apex of a week-long offering, not an isolated event. The daily altar of life reminds you that your true identity is forged not by market trends but by Christ's once-for-all act. In this way, your baptismal DNA pulses through every hour, calling you to live as a priestly conduit of God's grace.

9.1.2 Internalizing Righteousness and Extending Peace

The title "king of righteousness, king of peace" (Hebrews 7:2) describes Melchizedek's dual office and becomes your compass for personal formation. Internal righteousness begins with the daily practice of confession and renewal, acknowledging that your heart requires constant cleansing (Psalm 51:10). By inviting the Spirit to expose and transform inner patterns—pride, anger, indifference—you cultivate a disposition aligned with God's justice. Personal devotions anchored in Scripture—meditating on Micah 6:8's summons to "do justice, love mercy, walk humbly"—shape character more deeply than moralizing platitudes. Journaling prayers of lament and gratitude further inscribe divine peacemaking into your psyche, enabling you to carry calm amid anxiety. As righteousness becomes second nature internally, its fruit appears externally in acts of reconciliation—listening well, offering forgiveness, seeking restoration (Matthew 5:9). Extending peace then moves beyond platitudes into tangible hospitality: welcoming a lonely neighbor, advocating for the displaced, or facilitating dialogue across divides. In workplaces and communities, you become an agent of covenant shalom, reflecting Melchizedek's hospitality in Salem. When conflicts arise, you intercede—not as a passive bystander but as an active peacemaker empowered by inner righteousness. This dynamic interplay between inward transformation and outward ministry exemplifies the royal-priestly vocation you embrace. Living under the banner of righteousness and peace thus transforms both self and society, preparing you to establish daily rhythms of devotion.

9.2. Daily Rule of Life: Crafting Melchizedekian Rhythms

9.2.1 Dawn: Offering the First-Fruits of Attention

Beginning each day as an offering, you consecrate your first-fruits of attention to God, mirroring ancient agricultural worship where the best produce led the harvest (Proverbs 3:9). Before the world stirs, you pause in silence or brief prayer, acknowledging God's sovereignty over the coming hours. A simple morning liturgy—blessing the new day, reading Psalm 5 or 63—aligns your mind with divine priorities. Over coffee or a brief walk, you invite the Spirit to guide your thoughts, setting the tone for creative work and relationship.

This early devotion becomes a hinge on which the rest of your day turns, reminding you that your labor belongs first to the King-Priest. Technology can support this rhythm: reminder apps cue a breath prayer, devotional podcasts offer a psalm reading, and calendar annotations mark a "moment of Sabbath" at sunrise. You might keep a physical reminder—a lit candle or small bowl of water—to evoke baptismal consecration as you begin tasks. These dawn practices nourish the soul's well before external demands flood in, fostering resilience. They also establish you as one who lives in constant recognition of God's presence, rather than reactive to external stimuli. As dawn devotion shapes your orientation, so midday intercession emerges naturally as the next rhythmic act.

9.2.2 Mid-Day: Intercession in the Marketplace

At midday—the market's busiest season in biblical times— you step aside for intercession on behalf of your community, echoing Melchizedek's priestly advocacy. Whether in a short coffee break or a quick prayer walk, you lift up colleagues, neighbors, and national leaders, asking for wisdom, peace, and provision (1 Timothy 2:1). Carrying a small list—perhaps digitally—you pray for specific challenges: a coworker's health issue, local conflicts, systemic injustices. Such focused intercession enacts the priestly function of bearing others' burdens before the divine throne (Hebrews 4:16). You can practice listening prayer, pausing to sense the Spirit's guidance about whom to pray for and what to pray. Public prayer gatherings at lunchtime—either in person or online— can unify small groups in corporate petition, giving visible expression to the royal priesthood's solidarity. Even brief prayers of thanksgiving for provisions received remind you that daily bread is itself a divine gift (Matthew 6:11). This midday rhythm interrupts the centrifugal pull of self-concern, reorienting your heart toward cosmic priorities. As the sun reaches its zenith, so your prayers peak, preparing you to return to work with renewed perspective. The transition from intercession to evening covenant review then follows naturally, closing the daily liturgy of life.

9.2.3 Dusk: Covenant Review and Thanksgiving

As twilight descends, you perform a ritual of covenant review, recalling the day's events in light of God's faithfulness (Psalm 103:2). You revisit morning intentions and mid-day intercessions, noting answered prayers and areas requiring ongoing petition. This reflective practice might involve journaling, where gratitude entries and honest confessions create a ledger of grace and areas for growth. You can structure this review with a brief prayer guide—blessings, mistakes, learnings, hopes for tomorrow— anchoring each element in a question: "Where did I see God's righteousness? Where did I need to extend peace?" As darkness falls, you glimpse how your priest-king roles intertwined with life's fabric: instances of blessing, moments of conflict, channels of service. Concluding with thanksgiving—singing a short hymn like "Great Is Thy Faithfulness" or reciting Psalm 136's refrain—fosters an attitude of continual praise. Lighting a candle at the close of the day symbolizes Christ's undying presence, even into the night (John 8:12). This dusk ritual serves as both confession and benediction, ensuring you sleep in God's peace and awaken under His watch (Psalm 121:3). Through dawn, midday, and dusk, these daily rhythms embed Melchizedek's priestly-kingly pattern within the sacred arc of each 24-hour cycle, preparing you to reframe vocation as liturgy.

9.3. Vocation as Liturgy: Work Re-Imagined

9.3.1 Business Leadership under a Priestly Ethic

In corporate boardrooms, you carry the mantle of Melchizedek by integrating justice and mercy into decision-making. Leader-priests practice stewardship of resources, viewing profit not as an end but as a means to bless employees, communities, and stakeholders (Luke 16:9). Board meetings begin with a moment of invocation—praying for integrity, insight, and the welfare of all affected. Conflict resolution processes reflect covenant principles: listening deeply, seeking reconciliation, and crafting win-win solutions that promote dignity (Matthew 18:15–17). Ethical frameworks, such as triple bottom line accounting, measure people and planet alongside profit, embodying righteousness in corporate policy. Mentorship programs within companies train emerging leaders in servant leadership, modeling Christ's humility (Philippians 2:5–8). Business as mission projects link enterprises to gospel witness, employing local workers and reinvesting profits in social development. Workplace chapels or prayer rooms provide spaces for employees to pause, pray, and find spiritual refreshment during business hours. As a business leader, you cultivate a workplace culture of generosity, hosting regular "giving days" where employees volunteer their skills to nonprofits. Such practices transform commerce into covenant altar, where every transaction becomes an act of priestly service and royal stewardship. Through policies, practice, and prayer, the marketplace becomes a sacred venue for living in Melchizedek's order.

9.3.2 Healthcare, Teaching, and the Ministry of Healing

Hospitals and clinics become modern sanctuaries when healthcare professionals adopt a priestly approach to care. Doctors and nurses begin their shifts with silent prayer for patients, dedicating hands to God's healing ministry (James 5:14–15). Listening deeply to patient stories reflects Melchizedek's compassionate solidarity; it honors the image of God in every person. Ethical decision-making—regarding end-of-life care, allocation of scarce resources—follows principles of justice and mercy, ensuring the vulnerable receive priority. Pastoral care teams collaborate with medical staff, providing spiritual support alongside physical treatment, embodying holistic healing of body and soul (Luke 9:2). In schools, teachers become catechists, integrating moments of prayer, gratitude, and moral reflection into daily lessons, infusing education with covenant values. Educators champion inclusive practices, welcoming students of diverse backgrounds into learning communities rooted in belonging.

School chapels and assemblies open with Scripture readings that remind students of the King-Priest's call to love neighbor. Administrative policies—anti-bullying initiatives, equitable discipline—mirror Melchizedek's justice at the gate (Deuteronomy 16:18–20). By treating every learner as a royal priest-to-be, teachers foster a culture of mutual respect and spiritual formation. In both healthcare and education, vocation becomes liturgy—ministry that enacts Melchizedek's model of healing and teaching within contemporary institutions.

9.3.3 Creativity, Tech, and the Sanctification of Innovation

Artists, designers, and technologists join the royal-priestly vocation by consecrating creativity as a form of worship. Writers draw on biblical themes—bread and wine, covenant blessing—to craft narratives that invite audiences to encounter divine mystery. Musicians compose scores that incorporate ancient chant motifs into modern genres, uniting heritage and innovation. Visual artists create installations that evoke the Edenic banquet or heavenly liturgy, prompting viewers to ponder sacred realities. In tech, developers build apps that facilitate prayer rhythms—dawn, noon, dusk—integrating Melchizedekian patterns into daily life. Virtual reality experiences reconstruct biblical scenes—Melchizedek's meeting with Abraham or the heavenly throne room—immersing users in formative encounters. Hackathons and innovation labs dedicated to "faith tech" tackle social challenges—food insecurity, education gaps—as priestly service, deploying code for kingdom impact. Intellectual property policies can be shaped by covenant generosity, adopting open-source licensing to share breakthroughs for the common good. Tech leaders form "spiritual coding communities" that begin work sprints with a shared prayer, inviting wisdom beyond human algorithms. This sanctification of innovation reclaims creativity from mere entertainment, orienting it toward sacramental participation in God's redemptive work. By consecrating imagination and invention, lay and professional creatives embody Melchizedek's hidden yet potent ministry in the digital age.

9.4. Relational Hospitality: Bread-and-Wine Practices at Home

9.4.1 Family Tables, Shared Meals, and Storytelling

The home becomes a domestic sanctuary when weekly shared meals center on covenant remembrance, echoing Melchizedek's bread-and-wine hospitality. Families reserve a special day—Sabbath dinner or midweek supper—where all gather to bless the bread, pour the wine or juice, and recount God's faithfulness in personal stories (Deuteronomy 6:7). Children learn to ask, "Do you remember when…?" prompting older generations to pass down testimonies of divine provision. Table prayers incorporate Scripture: quoting Psalm 145:15–16 to acknowledge God as "the One who satisfies every living thing." Simple rituals—lighting a candle, reading a short devotion—imbue ordinary meals with sacred significance. Inviting neighbors or a lonely friend transforms a family supper into a mini-feast of peace, extending covenant hospitality beyond blood ties. Meal preparation becomes an act of service—priestly offering—where cooks pray over ingredients as first fruits. At the close, sharing leftovers with those in need enacts Melchizedek's generosity and Abram's tithe. Storytelling around the table trains memory and gratitude, linking familial love to divine covenants. Such practices forge deep relational bonds and model for children how faith is lived, not just taught. Over time, these table rites cultivate a household identity as a "royal priesthood," where every Sunday's corporate liturgy finds antidote in daily family worship. As domestic hospitality shapes the immediate circle, so outreach hospitality extends to strangers and strangers-to-be.

9.4.2 Welcoming Strangers, Refugees, and the Marginalized

Extending hospitality beyond the familiar family unit enacts Melchizedek's universal priesthood: Abraham welcomed a foreign king, and Christ embraced the outcast. Neighborhood potlucks intentionally invite newcomers and people of different cultures, creating spaces of intercultural exchange and mutual blessing. Refugee sponsorship programs facilitate adult language classes hosted in homes, turning living rooms into classrooms of grace. Community gardens on church grounds offer plots to marginalized families, ensuring access to healthy food and cultivating relationships through shared labor. Host homes organize "Open Table" meals for the homeless, breaking bread in solidarity rather than charity alone. Personal discomfort with social barriers becomes the soil for Intercultural Competency training, equipping hosts to listen and bridge differences. Local MIGROW (Migrant Integration Growth) networks connect hosts, mentors, and refugees in a structured welcome process, reflecting covenant patterns of allyship in Scripture (Leviticus 19:34). Sharing one's dwelling—even a couch—models the radical hospitality of Hebrews 13:2, which warns that some who have entertained angels unaware. Through these practices, homes become extension chapels of Melchizedek's Salem, offering sanctuary to the stranger. This relational hospitality transforms communities, modeling the shalom of the Kingdom in neighborhoods marked by division. As domestic and public hospitality entwine, the church's witness to the world deepens, demonstrating the lived reality of the Priest-King's welcome.

9.5. Kingdom Economics: Tithes, Generosity, and Jubilee Patterns

9.5.1 Budgeting as Worship

Every dollar you allocate becomes an act of worship when you recognize all resources as God's gift (1 Chronicles 29:14). Beginning each budgeting cycle with prayer frames your financial plan as obedience to the Priest-King's command rather than secular management. Setting aside a "first-fruit" percentage—echoing ancient Israel's tithe (Leviticus 27:30)—demonstrates trust that God will provide for all needs (Malachi 3:10). Allocating funds for local charities and global missions before personal spending inverts worldly priorities, placing

God's kingdom first (Matthew 6:33). Tracking expenses and income with transparency honors the biblical call to honest scales (Proverbs 11:1) and guards against temptation toward greed. Monthly "giving reviews" encourage gratitude by recalling answered prayers and enabling you to celebrate how generosity blessed others. Framing savings goals—emergency funds, education, retirement—as stewardship rather than hoarding aligns with Jesus's parable of the talents (Matthew 25:14–30). Regularly revisiting your budget in community—family, small group, accountability partner—embeds mutual encouragement and priestly intercession for financial faithfulness. Integrating a line item for Sabbath rest—days off, sabbatical savings—reflects Jubilee rhythms that release work's dominion (Leviticus 25:4). Electronic banking alerts can remind you of covenant pledges, ensuring tithes are automatically gifted. By worshipping through budgeting, every transaction proclaims that you serve a King who cares for both people and resources. This financial liturgy then flows into practices of debt forgiveness and micro-loan initiatives, the subject of the next subsection.

9.5.2 Debt-Release Initiatives and Micro-Loans

Following the Jubilee mandate to release debts every fifty years (Leviticus 25:10), Christians today can organize local debt-forgiveness drives for congregants and neighbors. Partnering with nonprofit credit-counseling agencies, churches host "Fresh Start" workshops where volunteers negotiate with creditors on behalf of low-income families. Micro-loan programs, modeled on biblical principles of solidarity (Acts 2:44–45), supply small business capital at zero or low interest, enabling entrepreneurs to flourish without predatory debt. Participants commit to peer accountability, mirroring Levitical community support in ancient Israel. Success stories—bakery owners, tailors, tech tutors—demonstrate how minor capital injections can catalyze dignity and kingdom impact. Grant and loan committees in churches follow transparent, prayer-filled discernment processes, ensuring decisions honor justice and mercy (Micah 6:8). Annual "Debt Sabbath" events encourage those who are able to forgive small personal debts, modeling Christ's call to forgive "seventy times seven" (Matthew 18:22). Reflection sessions explore how debt bondage echoes spiritual captivity, prompting corporate lament and intercession. Step-by-step financial literacy courses equip participants to avoid future pitfalls, weaving economic wisdom into discipleship. As forgiven debt frees people for service, micro-loan recipients often reinvest profits into community projects, multiplying kingdom impact. This cycle of release and empowerment enacts Melchizedek's covenant hospitality in economic structures, paving the way to ethical investing and creation care.

9.5.3 Ethical Investing and Creation Care

Investing as a priest-king practice means channeling capital into companies and funds that align with biblical values of justice, human dignity, and environmental stewardship (Genesis 2:15). Screening investments for fair labor practices, avoidance of weapons manufacturing, and sustainable resource use ensures your portfolio echoes covenant righteousness. Community investment funds pool small Christian investors to support local affordable housing, renewable energy, and minority-owned enterprises, reflecting Leviticus 25's vision of equitable land use. Impact bonds tied to social outcomes—job training, recidivism reduction, clean water access—offer measurable Kingdom dividends. Regular "investment sabbaticals" include prayer and research, inviting the Spirit's guidance rather than market hype. Conferences on faith-based investing foster peer learning, highlighting case studies of profitable enterprises that prioritize people over profit. Dividends and returns are partially tithed back into mission causes, closing the loop of covenant generosity. Shareholder advocacy campaigns engage corporate leadership on issues like climate justice and living wages, wielding Gospel influence in boardrooms. Education programs demystify terms like ESG (Environmental, Social, Governance) for congregants, equipping them to steward wealth responsibly. By combining financial acumen with priestly conscience, you transform your investments into vessels of righteous impact, transitioning us naturally into the sphere of public justice and advocacy.

9.6. Public Justice: Advocacy as Priest-King Duty

9.6.1 Grassroots Organizing for the Oppressed

Priestly advocacy begins at the grassroots, where you come alongside marginalized communities to amplify voices silenced by systemic injustice (Proverbs 31:8–9). Participating in neighborhood associations or forming advocacy task forces, you learn local histories, structural inequities, and the human stories behind statistics. Community listening sessions modeled on Acts 15's Jerusalem Council provide space for diverse stakeholders to share experiences without fear (Acts 15:6). Training in nonviolent direct action and strategic planning ensures that Christian advocacy remains both courageous and compassionate. Partnering with established nonprofits and local leaders avoids duplication of efforts and honors existing community wisdom. Policy research grounded in biblical ethics—drawing on Isaiah 1:17—equips you to propose legislative solutions that elevate the poor and protect the vulnerable. Mobilizing petition drives and letter-writing campaigns to elected officials enacts prophetic voices in civic life. Prayer vigils at sites of injustice—courthouses, detention centers—embody Melchizedek's intercession in the public square. Leadership teams of lawyers, pastors, and social workers collaborate to provide pro bono support for legal cases, reflecting Levitical care for the sojourner. Success stories—ordinances expanding affordable housing, anti-trafficking initiatives—demonstrate how priest-king advocacy yields tangible peace. As grassroots organizing builds relational trust, it lays the foundation for broader peacemaking in polarized societies.

9.6.2 Peacemaking in Polarized Societies

In an age of echo chambers and tribal conflict, Melchizedek's example of bridging political divides calls you to peacemaking initiatives grounded in empathy and justice. Dialogue circles bring together citizens of opposing views—racial, political, religious—for structured listening and storytelling, building trust brick by brick. Trained facilitators create safe spaces where participants agree to mutual respect, active listening, and confidential sharing. Scriptural anchors—Romans 12:18's call to "live peaceably as much as it depends on you"—guide these gatherings. Artistic collaborations—community murals, music events—enable nonverbal expressions of shared humanity. Joint service projects—cleaning parks, mentoring youth—forge partnerships through common purpose rather than debate. Local media and social platforms highlight stories of reconciliation, countering sensationalist divisiveness. Training programs in emotional intelligence and conflict transformation equip peacemakers to navigate interpersonal and structural tensions. Interfaith coalitions modeling Salem's multi-cultural hospitality extend peacemaking beyond Christian circles. Policy advocacy for restorative justice programs replaces punitive paradigms with healing modalities in criminal justice. Academic collaborations between divinity schools and peace studies centers generate research and training resources. Through these peacemaking efforts, you enact Melchizedek's vision of a kingdom where righteousness and peace converge, setting the stage for legislative engagement and civil disobedience.

9.6.3 Legislative Engagement and Civil Disobedience

When systemic injustice persists despite advocacy, priest-king duty may call for prophetic civil disobedience, modeled in Scripture by Shadrach, Meshach, and Abednego's refusal to worship idols (Daniel 3). Nonviolent protests—sit-ins, marches, fasting vigils—embody moral witness to laws that contradict God's higher law (Acts 5:29). Preparing for civil disobedience includes legal training, community support networks, and pastoral care for those who may face arrest. Prayer circles before and after actions sustain participants spiritually, reminding them that their ultimate allegiance is to God's kingdom. Testimonies given in public hearings and media interviews articulate theological convictions against unjust laws, appealing to universal human dignity. Lobbying legislators for policy repeal or reform continues alongside civil disobedience, combining inside and outside strategies. Historical examples—Martin Luther King Jr.'s civil rights movement, Bonhoeffer's resistance to Nazism—demonstrate the potent priestly-kingly fusion of moral courage and sacrificial love. As you engage legislative processes, you cultivate relationships with policymakers, offering expertise in crafting just laws. When laws lag behind justice, civil disobedience stands as the embodied prophecy of the eternal Priest-King who "comes to judge the earth" (Psalm 96:13). Through these dual modalities, you ensure that public justice remains both faithful to God's law and responsive to present human need.

9.7. Spiritual Warfare: Wearing the Royal Armor in Digital Spaces

9.7.1 Discernment, News Cycles, and Algorithmic Idols

 The digital realm has become a modern battlefield, where false narratives, polarization, and addictive content vie for human attention. As a royal priest, you wear the armor of truth by cultivating discernment through regular exposure to diverse, reliable news sources and rigorous fact-checking (Ephesians 6:14). Recognizing algorithmic idols—social media feeds that shape beliefs and emotions—you practice intentional media fasts, reclaiming your mind for spiritual reflection (Romans 12:2). Prayerful evaluation of trending topics prevents reactive indignation; instead, you ask, "What does gospel justice require here?" Digital discipleship groups host weekly "news prayer" sessions, where participants bring headlines before the throne in intercession and discernment. Devotional tools like the Examen can be adapted to review digital conduct: what content inspired love, what incited anger or fear? Learning the technical basics of platform algorithms empowers you to adjust settings, filter harmful content, and promote kingdom-oriented messages. Equipping children and youth with media literacy fosters resilient faith against digital temptations. Pastors model transparency about their own struggles with online time, inviting communal accountability. By treating digital engagement as spiritual terrain, you transform potential idols into opportunities for intercession and witness. This disciplined approach to the online sphere forms a bridge to the use of prayer-walk apps and virtual watchtowers in the next subsection.

9.7.2 Prayer-Walk Apps and Virtual Watchtowers

 Adapting ancient practices of city watchtowers (Habakkuk 2:1) to modern contexts, you use prayer-walk apps that map neighborhoods and send prayer prompts at designated points. As you physically walk through streets or scroll virtually through digital "maps," you pause to pray for homes, schools, and businesses, claiming spiritual guardianship. Augmented-reality overlays can display prayer requests from community databases at GPS locations, enabling targeted intercession for local needs. Prayer apps like *Pray As You Go* or *Echo* integrate Scripture prompts with location-based reminders, knitting prayer practices into daily routines. Virtual "watchtower" groups meet online for 24/7 prayer coverage, sharing intercession logs and encouraging one another in spiritual vigilance. Training resources equip participants to recognize spiritual strongholds—addiction, human trafficking hotspots—and pray strategically for their dismantling. Digital watchtowers also curate crisis alerts—natural disasters, civic unrest—mobilizing rapid prayer responses and material aid coordination. This fusion of technology and ancient spiritual practice enacts the royal-priestly mandate to stand in the gap for the city (Ezekiel 22:30). As you move between physical and virtual watchtowers, you personify the ever-present intercession of Christ, the eternal High Priest. These spiritual warfare tools prepare you to address the deeper needs of a wounded world in healing initiatives.

9.8. Healing and Wholeness: Charisms for a Wounded World

9.8.1 Listening Prayer, Trauma-Informed Care

Healing prayer begins with attentive listening—echoing James 1:19's injunction to be "quick to hear, slow to speak." Trained listening prayer teams create spaces where individuals share burdens without interruption, reflecting Melchizedek's compassionate solidarity (Hebrews 5:2). Learning basic trauma-informed principles—safety, choice, collaboration—ensures that prayer spaces do not re-traumatize the vulnerable. Scripture passages like Psalm 147:3 ("He heals the brokenhearted") become anchors for prayer of lament and hope. Prayer ministers use simple rituals—laying on of hands, anointing with oil, recitation of healing Scriptures—to embody God's healing touch (Mark 6:13). Follow-up care plans link pray-ers to counseling, support groups, and community resources, integrating spiritual and professional care. Debrief sessions help intercessors process emotional burdens and maintain healthy boundaries. Regular training in emotional intelligence equips teams to discern when to refer to mental health professionals. Creative arts therapies—drawing, music, movement—offer alternative pathways to express pain and experience wholeness. Case studies—survivors of abuse, veterans with PTSD—highlight how integrated care honors both spiritual and psychological dimensions. By combining charisms of empathy, discernment, and prophetic blessing, healing ministries manifest Melchizedek's timeless intercession for God's people.

9.8.2 Community Gardens and Embodied Shalom

Community gardens transform urban lots into living laboratories of embodied shalom, weaving theology, ecology, and social justice. As gardeners cultivate soil, plant seeds, and harvest produce, they enact Genesis 2:15's mandate to "tend and keep" creation under God's dominion. Shared plots function as priestly altars where people of diverse backgrounds—income levels, ethnicities, ages—labor side by side in covenant solidarity. Produce gleaned from excess yields feeds food pantries, addressing local hunger with dignity rather than handouts alone. Garden churches hold "harvest feasts," inviting neighbors to break bread amid the very fruits of communal labor, echoing Melchizedek's covenant meal (Genesis 14:18). Ecological stewardship practices—composting, rainwater harvesting, pollinator plantings—demonstrate care for creation as part of God's temple (Revelation 11:19). Educational workshops connect biblical Creation narratives to practical gardening skills, fostering intergenerational learning. Art installations—mosaics of Psalm 104 scenes—link worship space and garden, reminding volunteers that nature itself praises the Creator. Seasonal rhythms—planting in spring, harvesting in fall—align with liturgical calendars of Easter and Thanksgiving, embedding liturgy in land. Through community gardens, healing of bodies, relationships, and the land converges, offering a microcosm of Melchizedek's integrated reign. This embodied shalom catalyzes neighborhood renewal, demonstrating that priest-king ministry begins in the mud beneath our feet.

9.9. Missional Networks: Micro-Churches and Marketplace Chapels

9.9.1 Start-Up Hubs as Mission Fields

In city centers and innovation districts, start-up incubators and co-working spaces offer fertile ground for micro-church planting, reflecting Melchizedek's unconventional kingdom venues. Entrepreneurs gather around shared tables—coffee bars, ping-pong tables, brainstorming walls—creating organic opportunities for covenant hospitality (Acts 2:44–47). Believers who work in these hubs can host short "huddle chapels" at lunch, offering five-minute devotionals and prayer for projects and people. The integration of prayer stations—

simple symbols of bread and cup—into communal lounges invites anyone to pause and pray in the midst of business pitches. Online platforms for hub members can include a dedicated "Marketplace Chapel" channel with Scripture reflections and prayer requests. Start-ups focused on social impact find natural synergy with Melchizedekian values of justice and peace, enabling peer mentorship circles that blend business coaching with spiritual formation. Office décor can feature art invoking covenant symbolism—a canvas of Melchizedek blessing Abram—reminding innovators of kingdom priorities. Biweekly "learning liturgies" can frame design sprints and hackathons as acts of creative stewardship under God's rule (Genesis 1:28). These gatherings employ brief creeds or affirmations to unite diverse founders under shared convictions. When funding cycles begin, prayer for investors and ethical decision-making invites divine wisdom into pitch rooms. By repurposing start-up culture's love of community into mission networks, believers live out Melchizedek's order in the marketplace, transitioning naturally into sports and arts venues as additional chapels of mission.

9.9.2 Sports, Arts, and Third-Place Gatherings

Stadiums, galleries, and cafés—so-called "third places"— serve as contemporary community centers where believers can incarnate covenant hospitality. Sports ministries host pickup basketball or soccer games followed by brief devotionals under portable communion tables, blending physical exertion with spiritual refreshment (1 Corinthians 9:24–27). Artists' collectives can open gallery nights where paintings and installations depict scriptural narratives— Melchizedek's blessing, Christ's priestly intercession— sparking conversations about faith and beauty. Local cafés offer "poetry chapels" where spoken-word artists explore themes of justice and mercy, echoing Psalm 107's call to "let the redeemed of the Lord say so." Open-mic worship nights invite musicians to improvise hymns and spiritual songs, connecting diverse genres under the Melchizedekian banner of praise. Community theater troupes can stage short plays based on Genesis 14, re-enacting the bread-and-wine encounter as a catalyst for dialogue on hospitality and covenant. Book clubs, TEDx-style talks, and pop-up prayer booths in parks become venues for sharing personal testimonies of God's provision. Street art tours highlight faith-inspired murals and provide accompaniment to local artists, framing urban creativity as divine partnership. Each sporting event, exhibition, or gathering transforms secular space into a mission chapel where those unaccustomed to church can experience kingdom values incarnationally. As these third-place worship forms flourish, practitioners gain skills that feed back into formal church planting and faith communities.

9.10. Intergenerational Formation: Passing the Scepter

9.10.1 Mentoring, Apprenticeship, and Story-Circles

Intergenerational formation recaptures the apprenticeships of biblical settings—Elijah and Elisha, Paul and Timothy—by creating mentoring relationships that pass spiritual inheritance. Seasoned believers ("elders" in the New Testament sense) commit to mentor younger Christians through regular one-on-one meetings, focusing on scriptural study, vocational discernment, and character formation (2 Timothy 2:2). Apprenticeship cohorts gather in "story-circles" where each generation shares testimonies of God's faithfulness, creating a living archive of covenant memory. These circles use the ancient practice of oral storytelling to internalize lessons from fields as varied as farming, entrepreneurship, and ministry. Structured "scepter handovers" at the close of each apprenticeship year symbolically pass leadership roles—prayer, liturgy, community care—to the next generation. Reflection guides rooted in Hebrews 13:7 prompt mentees to consider how their mentors imitated the faith that now guides them. Communities invite grandparents into Sunday school classes and youth retreats, enabling reciprocal teaching where elders learn digital skills through "reverse mentoring." This relational network establishes a fabric of accountability, wisdom, and innovation that mirrors Melchizedek's timeless priesthood moved forward by fresh hands. The momentum from mentoring and story-circles sets the stage for digital catechesis, integrating technology into intergenerational formation.

10.2 Digital Catechesis and Reverse Mentoring

Digital catechesis leverages online platforms—learning management systems, video series, podcasts—to deliver foundational teaching on Melchizedek's order to dispersed generations. Bite-sized modules on typology, liturgy, and priesthood integrate videos, quizzes, and discussion boards, enabling busy learners to engage at their own pace. Virtual small groups led by seasoned theologians facilitate live Q&A sessions and prayer support. Meanwhile, "reverse mentoring" invites tech-savvy younger believers to guide older Christians through digital tools—social media, collaboration software, virtual reality worship—ensuring that tradition and innovation advance hand in hand. This reciprocal model fosters humility and mutual learning, akin to Christ's servant-master dynamics (Mark 10:45). Churches create digital archives of recorded sermons, panel discussions, and worship sessions on platforms accessible to all generations. Mobile apps send daily prompts for theological reflection or liturgical prayer at dawn, noon, and dusk, reinforcing daily rule practices. Intergenerational online hackathons tackle real-world problems—food shortage, climate justice—grounded in Melchizedekian ethics, uniting ages in mission. Online mentoring pairs rural and urban congregants, bridging geographic and cultural gaps in shared discipleship. By integrating digital catechesis and reverse mentoring, the church ensures that every generation both receives and reshapes the legacy of the eternal Priest-King.

11. Metrics of Faithfulness: Evaluating Impact without Idolatry

11.1 Fruit of the Spirit over Followers and Funds

Quantitative metrics—attendance numbers, budget size—risk becoming idols when they eclipse qualitative measures of spiritual health. Instead, churches adopt fruit-focused metrics based on Galatians 5:22–23, evaluating love, joy, peace, patience, kindness, goodness, faithfulness, gentleness, and self-control in community life. Small group check-ins include self-assessment of fruit presence, prompting personal and communal reflection. Leadership development programs track mentee growth in these virtues rather than numeric targets alone. Annual ministry reviews incorporate testimonies of changed lives—stories of reconciliation, healing, and spiritual breakthrough—as primary success indicators. Surveys among outreach recipients assess whether acts of service conveyed dignity and compassion, rather than simply counting meals served. Staff performance reviews emphasize servant leadership traits—humility, empathy, integrity—over fund-raising totals. Board dashboards display fruit metrics alongside financial reports, reminding decision-makers that profits serve kingdom priorities. This fruit-centered approach resists the temptation to pursue growth at any cost, anchoring mission in Christlike character. As fruit metrics reveal spiritual vitality, the church transitions to narrative reporting and communal discernment as deeper evaluation methods.

11.2 Narrative Reporting and Communal Discernment

Narrative reporting embraces storytelling as a primary means of evaluating ministry impact, capturing nuance and context that numbers miss. Churches collect "ministry stories" through video interviews, written testimonies, and photo essays, assembling digital portfolios of kingdom impact. Quarterly "discernment retreats" gather leaders and stakeholders to review stories in light of Scripture and Spirit-prompted

218

insights, discerning next steps together. Storyboards displayed in communal spaces remind congregants of milestones—healing journeys, advocacy victories, worship innovations. Decision-making processes leverage discernment practices—prayerful silence, lectio divina on guiding passages, resonance checks—so that future initiatives align with God's direction rather than organizational ambition (Acts 13:2–3). Annual "Ministry Narrative Books" summarize key stories, reflect on lessons learned, and outline vision for the coming year, integrating contributions from staff, volunteers, and beneficiaries. These narrative reports become teaching tools in Sunday school and catechumen classes, weaving evaluation into formation. By privileging stories, the church honors the complexity of human transformation and the mysterious work of the Spirit. This communal discernment approach transitions naturally into the eschatological hope that sustains perseverance.

12. Horizon of Hope: Awaiting the City of Peace

12.1 Sabbath as Prophetic Protest

Observing Sabbath becomes a counter-cultural proclamation that God—not productivity—is the ultimate source of life and blessing (Exodus 20:8–11). Choosing rest on the seventh day stands as prophetic protest against the capitalist idol of constant work, affirming trust in divine provision. Families who practice Sabbath meals disconnect from screens, invitations, and errands, creating space for worship, play, and relational restoration. Congregations host community Sabbaths—public parks, shared hikes, collective picnics—inviting the broader public to sample rhythms of kingdom rest. Digital sabbath initiatives encourage churches and businesses to go offline simultaneously, modeling a society that honors sacred time. Reflecting on Sabbath rest in pastoral prayers reminds believers that their final Sabbath awaits in the City of God (Hebrews 4:9). Teaching on Sabbath hospitality—welcoming strangers to rest—echoes Melchizedek's bread-and-wine welcome, expanding rest into communal care. Journaling sabbath experiences cultivates awareness of Sabbath's restorative power, offering qualitative "rest metrics" for spiritual health. This Sabbath as prophetic protest points beyond liturgical forms to a future hope where no labor or longing remains (Revelation 14:13), transitioning hearts toward vigilant expectation.

12.2 Vigilant Expectation and the Maranatha Cry

Living in the order of Melchizedek includes watching and waiting for the consummation of all things, echoing Revelation 22:20's Maranatha—"Come, Lord Jesus!" Such vigilant expectation shapes daily posture: prayer meetings often close with this cry, aligning congregational hope with cosmic fulfillment. Regular "vigil services" at dawn or midnight recall early Christian traditions of watchfulness, integrating prayer, silence, and hymnody. Personal practices—keeping a "memory box" of promises and answered prayers—sustain hope when circumstances press hard. Corporate reading of apocalyptic texts—Daniel 7, Revelation 21—paired with art reflections, embeds eschatological vision in communal imagination. Annual Advent retreats focus on "in-between" living, preparing hearts for both Christ's first coming and His return. Community lament services acknowledge pain and injustice, yet conclude with songs of future glory, demonstrating faith that hope transcends present suffering (Romans 8:18–25). Mission strategies incorporate eschatological urgency, motivating witnesses to "make disciples of all nations" while time allows (Matthew 28:19). Teaching on perseverance, drawn from Hebrews 12:1–2, encourages believers to "run with endurance" toward the city of peace. This vigilant expectation keeps the royal-priestly calling dynamic, vibrant, and forward-looking, ensuring that all practices—worship, work, justice—point to the living King who reigns forever.

Conclusion

Embracing life in Melchizedek's order transforms ordinary days into a living sacrament, where every act of justice, every shared loaf, and every prayer for the hurting becomes a thread in God's unfolding story of peace. As you steward resources with jubilee-minded generosity, pursue justice with kingly compassion, and pray with priestly persistence, you join a global chorus of worshipers whose hope is anchored in an eternal covenant (1 Peter 2:9; Revelation 5:10). This royal-priestly vocation resists idols of productivity and power, calling you instead to Sabbath rhythms that testify to God's ultimate rest and renewal. Living in Melchizedek's order today means anticipating—and advancing—the day when the Lord God and the Lamb alone will be our temple and reign forever (Revelation 21:22–23). In that hope, Christians everywhere rehearse now the peaceable kingdom yet to come.

www.ingramcontent.com/pod-product-compliance
Lightning Source LLC
Chambersburg PA
CBHW060317050426
42449CB00011B/2524